George Szirtes

REEL

BLOODAXE BOOKS

Copyright © George Szirtes 2004

ISBN: 1 85224 676 6

First published 2004 by
Bloodaxe Books Ltd,
Highgreen,
Tarset,
Northumberland NE48 1RP.

Second impression 2005.

www.bloodaxebooks.com
For further information about Bloodaxe titles
please visit our website or write to
the above address for a catalogue.

Bloodaxe Books Ltd acknowledges
the financial assistance of
Arts Council England, North East.

Cover printing by J. Thomson Colour Printers Ltd, Glasgow.

Printed in Great Britain by
Bell & Bain Limited, Glasgow, Scotland.

REEL

George Szirtes was born in Budapest in 1948, arrived in England as a refugee in 1956 and was brought up in London. He was trained as a painter in Leeds and at Goldsmiths College. He has taught art, history of art and creative writing in various schools and colleges, and currently teaches poetry and creative writing at the Norwich School of Art and Design and the University of East Anglia. For some years he exhibited and ran a small etching and poetry press together with his wife, artist Clarissa Upchurch. Their children, Tom and Helen, were born and grew up in Hertfordshire.

His poems began to appear in print in the mid 70s. His first book, *The Slant Door*, was awarded the Geoffrey Faber Prize and since then he has won the Cholmondeley Award and been short-listed for the Whitbread and Forward Poetry Prizes. He was elected a Fellow of the Royal Society of Literature in 1982.

After his first return to Hungary in 1984 he translated poetry, fiction and plays from the Hungarian and for his work in this field he has won the European Poetry Translation Prize, the Dery Prize and been shortlisted for the Weidenfeld and Aristeion Prizes as well as receiving the Golden Star medal of the Hungarian republic. He co-edited Bloodaxe's *The Colonnade of Teeth: Modern Hungarian Poetry* (1996) with George Gömöri, and his Bloodaxe edition of Ágnes Nemes Nagy's poetry, *The Night of Akhenaton: Selected Poems* (2004), was a Poetry Book Society Recommended Translation. His study of the artist Ana Maria Pacheco, *Exercise of Power*, was published by Ashgate in 2001. He has also written for children, and is currently working on a novel about wrestling.

Much of his poetry has been collected in two selections from Bloodaxe, *The Budapest File* (2000) and *An English Apocalypse* (2001). His latest collection from Bloodaxe, *Reel* (2004), was a Poetry Book Society Choice and won the 2004 T.S. Eliot Prize. He reads a half-hour selection of his work on *The Poetry Quartets 6* (The British Council/Bloodaxe Books, 2000), a double-cassette shared with Moniza Alvi, Michael Donaghy and Anne Stevenson.

To the ghost of childhood
and the body of the adult

'To watch is possible: therefore you must watch.'

MARTIN BELL: 'Ode to Himself'

ACKNOWLEDGEMENTS

Acknowledgements are due to the editors of the following publications where some of these poems first appeared: *Ambit*, *Being Alive* (Bloodaxe Books, 2004), *The Gift: New Writing for the NHS* (Stride, 2002), *The Hudson Review* (USA), *Hungarian Quarterly*, *Kenyon Review* (USA), *London Magazine*, *Maisonnerve* (Canada), *Metre*, *New Writing 8* (Vintage / British Council, 1999), *Poetry Review*, *Poetry Wales*, *The Rialto*, *The Shop* (Ireland), *Short Fuse* (Rattapallax Press, 2002), *The Times* and *Tri Quarterly* (USA). All five poems in the series 'My Fathers' first appeared in *Poetry* (USA).

'Preface to an Exhibition', 'The Wicked Boy by the Pylons' and 'Water' were commissioned by the Barbican Art Gallery for their Sebastião Salgado exhibition.

CONTENTS

ACCOUNTS

Reel

(for Clarissa Upchurch)

1

You wake to car sounds, radios, the cold sunlight
Burning holes in windows, and you sense
The missing fabric of the previous night.

The city offers you no evidence
Except the collage of the overheard,
Extended clauses of a broken sentence

Of which you recognise the odd stray word.
A car door slams. Feet scutter down the stairs.
It is the Theatre of the Absurd,

A masquerade in which the company wears
Period dress, their every movement fragile,
Negotiating brittle stools and chairs.

Eclectic, Art Deco, Secession style
Buildings multiply into a capital
Of iron, bronze, glass brick, ceramic tile.

A statue balanced on a pedestal
Is leaning over to whisper a close secret.
Two yellow trams clatter in mechanical

Circles. Dull monuments express regret
For what someone has done to them, for crimes
Committed in names they're trying to forget

But can't. Here all the clocks tell different times.
All the statues point different ways. Film crews
Shoot Budapest for Berlin. The city rhymes

With its imperial neighbour, like one bruise
With another. People converge on streets
Where there is never any lack of news.

Here is a square where everybody meets.
Here is a doorway through which troops have pressed.
Here is a yard with women hanging sheets

And corridors where boys in Sunday best
Are waiting for a housekeeper or maid
To join them on a stroll in the soft west

Wind ruffling the embankment trees. Decade
After decade resolves itself in the traffic.
The filming goes on somewhere in the shade.

2

Once you arrive in the heart of the exotic,
Which is only a transferred idea of home,
Under the crumbling stucco, the faint brick

Of memory appears. Above the lanterned dome
Of the cathedral the familiar sky
Waves back, reflected in the brilliant chrome

Of legions of saloon cars purring by.
It is as if they drove some narrative
Whose visual sub-plot struck your painter's eye

With its peculiar imperative.
Even the light here has grown eloquent,
Its language sparklingly authoritative.

The city glories in its element.
I woke here as a child once in a narrow
Bedroom that served as my Old Testament.

Like a philosopher I watched Time's arrow
Winging towards its target and falling short.
So God is said to note a falling sparrow...

Genesis, Exodus... it was a fishing port,
An English holiday town, time blew me to,
Where I could watch waves, like immortals, sport

With bits of flotsam once the wind was through.
Here I find lost bits of my heart. In these
Dark corridors and courtyards something true

Survives in such obsessive images
As understand the curtains of the soul
Drawing together in the frozen breeze.

And you, born in the Far East, in a bowl
Of China dust, carried in armoured trucks
Along Malaysian roads, and down the coal-

Seamed valleys of Yorkshire, past viaducts
And airports, can now enter through the walls
To haunt the darkest residential blocks.

3

What hope for rhyme when even childhood calls
On fiction for an echo and completes
Itself in myths, processions, carnivals,

Displays that billow down mysterious streets?
The city is unfixed, its formal maps
Are mere mnenomics where each shape repeats

Its name before some ultimate collapse.
The train shunts in the sidings, cars pull in
By doorways, move off, disappear in gaps

Between the shops. It is like watching skin
Crack and wrinkle. Old words: *Andrássy út*
And *Hal tér*. Naming of streets: *Tolbuhin,*

Münnich... the distant smell of rotting fruit,
Old shredded documents in blackened piles,
Dead trees with squirrels snuffling at the root.

On balmy afternoons you walk for miles
Trying to listen to the architecture.
It mutters continually, waving dusty files

Of unsolved grievances. It wants to lecture
Even while it sings – and how it sings,
When the mood takes it! So you take its picture

And brood upon those mouths and eyes, the wings
Of its cracked angels and draw out the sound
In terms of light which darkens as it rings.

Bells of the city chime, round upon round.
The film rolls on. A car sweeeps round the bend,
Its shadow stripping grey from the pale ground.

4

Sooner or later roads come to an end.
The tram draws to a stop beside the bridge
Then doubles back. Cogwheel railways descend

To their terminus. You reach the world's edge
To leap off or to turn around and face
The ardours of the tiring homeward trudge.

The beggars in the subway know their place.
The shopgirl yawns. A couple in the square
Seem to be locked in statuesque embrace.

Surely by now the credits should appear.
Our characters, our narratives, our themes
And leitmotifs are hanging in the air

As dusk comes on with the small print of dreams.
We get into the car and cruise away
Negotiating networks of dipped beams.

Everything snores. Even the fine spray
Of rain breathes evenly. The houses close
Their doors to the street. Bedroom curtains sway

And darken. Somewhere in the comatose
Suburbs two people chase each other through
Sequences of courtyards with black windows.

Today is history, only the night is new
And always startling. Slowly the paint flakes
On the wall. Eventually the film-crew

Pack their gear away. The darkness aches
For morning which arrives with bird-calls, gusts
Of wind and traffic just as the reel breaks.

Meeting Austerlitz

(i.m. W.G. Sebald)

DECEMBER 2001

1

The cold sat down with frozen fingers. Cars
were iced up, the pavements were treacherous.
Boys in t-shirts drifted through doors of bars

in quiet market towns. The shops were a chorus
of seasonal favourites, every one the same.
We were jollying ourselves up for Christmas

without much money and no sense of shame
because this was a time for giving and for joy.
We were all good intentions. So the postman came

and went, lorries delivered supplies, the boy
with the papers zipped about on his bike,
parents were packing the latest must-have toy,

(each one expensive, every one alike),
the butcher's whole family were busy serving
and no one had fallen ill or gone on strike.

On ungritted roads motorists were swerving
to avoid each other. Nothing had come to bits
in the houses of the whole and the wholly deserving,

nothing was incomprehensible or beyond our wits
and I myself was taking a quiet stroll
in the nearby fields when I met Austerlitz.

It was some way off the road and he was the sole
patch of dark in the bright mid-afternoon.
Hello Max, I said. And he looked up with that droll

melancholy expression. There was the faintest moon
visible in the sky. *Both day and night,*
he grinned. *It'll be dusk pretty soon.*

17

In Lalla Rookh, *if I remember right,*
I've not read Thomas Moore for several years,
there's a veiled prophet, Hakim, who radiates light

and draws the moon from a well. When it appears
it eclipses the real moon. Perhaps we have invented
the sad pale thing there with its terrible shears.

The air was frosty, oddly tobacco-scented,
thick grey clouds rose from his mouth as he spoke.
I could not be certain whether the wisps that entered

my mouth were frozen breath or cigarette smoke:
everything had a double or existed
in some version of itself wrapped in a winter cloak.

It was as if an enormous window had misted.
Austerlitz was looking across the field.
Beyond the window, there were buildings twisted

into macabre shapes. Some creature squealed
in the distance. A car growled briefly past.
Then silence, complete and vacuum-sealed.

2

I could not believe that Austerlitz was dead.
Though others had died that year his death was strange.
His voice had internalised itself in my head

and I kept listening to see how it would arrange
the furniture it found there. Certainly
it would improve things. Almost any change

would do that. A puff of dust from the library,
swirling like ashes, had settled across his prose,
its flavour tart, magical and scholarly,

as tired as the world. Each cadence had to close
on what remained of it. A collection of postcards,
a guidebook, a street-map. The attempt to impose

order was a perilous task, all but beyond words
while the alternative universe of flux
offered no sympathy and kept no records.

His were meticulous, a kind of *fiat lux*
compounded of atoms. My mind being a mess
I wanted his vision blowing through the ducts.

Though Austerlitz had died the tenderness
of his precision was consoling. No one
could start at quite that angle to the homeless

intellect. It was the winter sun.
His voice moved in the frozen field and I
would follow it and beg him to carry on.

3

I was writing about wrestlers. There were books
and videos and interviews. I thought
long about the body, the way it looks

and functions, the way the body fought
its enemies – other bodies, disease,
the weather, the impossible onslaught

of information, and the curious sleaze
it took to – but also its courage, miraculous
cogency and ability to please.

My half-century had passed. I was feckless
and wanted to listen to what Austerlitz
might say on the subject, however ridiculous.

I knew a good man once, of regular habits,
he began, *a doctor, who lived just there*
beyond the field. In reasonable spirits

you'd have thought. It was a bad affair,
a long way from his birthplace. He was ill
of course, but others sicken without despair

quite breaking through like that. We can distil
our terrors and make them hang like a grey mist
beyond the garden, somehow peripheral,

and I considered him an optimist
compared to me, though that's a matter of style.
Body and mind, the way they co-exist,

is by breeding madness which festers a while
but sooner or later starts jabbering, and then
at last it is as if an imbecile

had always possessed you. Your wrestling men
are like the demons that Jesus exorcised,
playing at swine herded into a pen

or ring, and we pretend to be surprised
when they break free and tumble from a height.
Demons are inevitably oversized

by our usual standards. We remain polite,
value nobility, and the poor doctor was the most
courteous of people until that night.

Things just add up, especially the lost
things. He breathed out and the air stood still
before it vanished slowly like a ghost.

4

But I was not prepared to let him go
so easily. I knew that in his mind
there was a tendency to counter-flow

and double exposure. He would unwind
the world of memory and wind it up again
a little off-centre as though it were a blind

or hedge against bad luck. *You can't explain*
history to itself, he said. *It has*
neither ears nor eyes. Humankind must train

itself to refocus or employ mirrors.
That morning I had leaned forward to shave
and thought to see myself in my true colours,

but the face was broader and I seemed to have
no focal point at all. The nose was there,
and eyes, ears, mouth, chin, cheeks, but nothing gave

the parts coherence. The face was just too bare,
I could not glimpse it as another could
in another dimension, less self-aware.

I remembered my mother's face in childhood,
my father's worried look, my children's deep
otherness, my wife's eyes, and saw the blood

that ran through all of us like dreams in sleep
in faint streams of reality, a secret plumbing
telling us who we were, what we could keep

and what we'd have to lose in whatever was coming.
But we were standing still in the stiff grass.
It was almost dusk and the cold was numbing.

Perhaps we were statues and time would pass
leaving us unaltered, or him at least.
His words were turning to silver behind glass

like any mirror, although the mouth had ceased
moving and his breath was only in my head
stirred by a wind directly north-north-east.

5

We're born in joy, we live joy and we die
into joy, say the masses crowding on the shore
of the Ganges. *You listen to the cry*

of the holy men, said Austerlitz. *The more
they cry, the greater the joy. You speak the name
of the god and it appears in shadows on the floor*

*or in the seeds of a plant, everywhere the same.
But names are like dreams we disappear into
where all things seem to fit into the frame*

*of their narrative. It is names we journey through:
they're landscapes of what ever happens and goes
on happening as we progress, neither old nor new.*

*Take photographs, the way a flashbulb blows
your swollen shadow up against the wall
behind you. A momentary perception grows*

*into an image. It is an oddly comical
sensation. Frozen motion. Blind field.* I stared
at the panoramic photograph of my old school

seeking my younger face, darker and thicker haired
lost cousin among all the faces trapped
in the moment. It was, I think, time that shared

us, not us that did the sharing, however rapt
the attention the camera gave us. We were stopped
in our tracks by it as if time itself had snapped

shut. We were part of something that was cropped
and stern but opened out again into time
that carried on either side of the camera propped

on its tripod. Look how our mouths mime
to the words we are speaking now. *It is late,*
said Austerlitz, watching the stars climb

to their stations. *The gods of joy can wait
forever, and so can we.* It was cold. I stood
trembling beside him, trying to concentrate

as the fields disappeared into the wood,
till my own image hung for a second then went
absent, not for a moment but for good.

He too watched it go, then slowly bent
his head and leaned it on my shoulder, as he had
the last time we had met, like a penitent,

and I was touched. It was terribly sad
to think of it. A car was drifting by
as in an old film. I took the nearby road

back into town just as snow began to fly.
Christmas lights dripped from windows winking
their enormous eyes at the dark sky.

6

We'd met at the station once, in the café.
It was cold then too, both of us shivering
and we said hello to each other then moved away.

I saw the crippled bushes weathering
with dead traveller's joy. At Manningtree
quicksilver mudflats and channels feathering

water with light, a water-tower, the Marconi
factory at Chelmsford. The whole train-
ride was a kind of speculative journey

into melancholy in a steady rain
of terraced houses, the imperium
of the great city spreading like a stain

across suburbs, from village to reclaimed slum
in three generations. The great hotels
at the terminus, spire and dome and drum,

were ghost planets of marble and precious metals,
metaphors for a solar system whose core
had disintegrated in a peal of bells

echoing forever along one shore
or another. Water ate away each edifice,
both centre and periphery. The roar

of crumbling brickwork and the shriek of ice
in the North Sea. Gulls swirling in a high
circle over pigeons, terrace on terrace

like slow waves. I saw you pulling your wry
face again. The place was grim. I sat down
nursing my coffee and a piece of dry

Danish pastry. You'd vanished into town,
and I waited for my train and played with the sugar,
holding a lump in my spoon, letting it drown.

7

My bookmark is a little headed note:
the Esperia Hotel in Athens. The room
looked out on a side street which seemed to float

in an almost permanent state of gloom
and only when the sun rose to noon height
did it penetrate there beyond the boom

of traffic at the front where all the light
available had gathered. The TV showed
a micro-second of hard porn as bait:

a tongue, a vulva, a thrusting groin, glowed
then disappeared. Something silky froze
into permanence, in an elsewhere you could decode

with a machine. *So a piece of silk could close*
the gap between worlds, Austerlitz observed,
quoting somebody. *The picture that shows*

the young girl in the garden, her lips faintly curved
into a smile, is touching because she is lovely
and gone. Going is what we have deserved

and welcomed. The puzzled small dog on her knee,
the doll at her feet, the bent-wood chair, the flowers
behind her are silky cellulose. Photography

has made them into dwarfish ghosts, sleek showers
of light beating down an endless slope.
My feet are sliding even now. There are a few hours

left, if that. The bookmark remains. The soap
by the basin. The towels. The curtains. The name
of the hotel, which, as you know, means hope.

Noir

With a firm hand, she dabs at two pink pancakes
and smooths herself right out. The man next door
crushes his cigarette in the ashtray and makes

a call. A car draws up below. There are more
cars by the curbside, waiting with lights on.
Everything is ready. Lights on the floor

above snap off. Whatever business was being done
is done. It's time for bed. Boys stir in sleep
to the sounds of drumming that might be a handgun.

The plot is too complex and runs too deep
for neat solutions. There are only cars
and endless cruising. There are secrets you keep

and secrets you don't yet know. There are scars
below scars and, eventually, daylight over the hill
to wipe the windscreens by the all-night bars

but shadows remain on the lung and the grille
of the sedan parked by the gate. What troubles you?
Why so anxious? Why do you stand so still?

Sheringham

When you come out of the sea, with its faint
illegible scrawl of scum like a smudged sleeve,
you hear the screak of pebbles sucked slant

under and round, and begin at last to believe
in the longer perspectives of geological
time, hearing its music as if each semibreve

of stone added up to a monumental
composition that went on dissolving
even as it sounded, out of your control;

so steeply shelving banks of grey stone sing
to one another, as if they had a voice
that was slowly but perfectly evolving

out of itself into a human face.
Once on a website I saw a man rise
out of a crowd of old scholars. It was Chris

Coles who played football with me. His eyes
were exactly as they had been, though the hair
was grey like the beachstones and his nose

seemed broader perhaps but I could see, somewhere
at the back of it, his old nose and chin
like a shadow on the steady coastal air

until a wave broke and the old face slid back in
under the new one which, I guess, had shocked me.
It shocked because both images were thin,

thinner than I had expected and so exactly
matched in the way the waves had rinsed them clean.
When I was twenty I worked in a factory

attending a boiler-sized plastic-tube machine
that spewed curved pipes at regular intervals,
which I had to file down and throw in a waiting bin.

And Chris, where was he then? On what thermals
was he billowing onward? He had been half-back
and captain too, tackling and knocking long balls

out to the wings where I was waiting to attack,
to centre or cut in, and the rain was falling hard
on the dark green and brown grass which was slick

as spittle, where enthusiasm was its own reward.
Chris was in his world, and I was stuck in mine,
except for the match after which we'd board

the school bus and go home and the rain
was still falling. We had our desks at school,
our friends, our 'A' Levels. So it would go on

changing under the rain, down a long spool
of cloud that thinned, thickened or vanished
as sun broke through. It was a miracle,

all of it, the long walls of time that crashed
about our ears without crushing us. And always
these visits to the seaside and its embellished

cuffs of water, rubbing away whole days.
I watched a toddler in a red quilted jacket
teeter down stones making tiny forays

onto the black, wet, still sucked-and-licked
lowest tier of them, seeing time itself
contract into a child in the vast derelict

expanse of the sea that swallowed up each shelf,
and the expensive beach-huts with their locks
and curtains above, one with its door half-

open to the wind, and all the silent clocks
of the digital age moving forward together
with Chris Coles and I in a mathematics

far beyond my own and, beyond us, all the other
boiled down particulars that regularly come
knocking at the skull in the blank weather

and this terrible word, love, the only sum
we can think of adding to the loneliness
to make up the difference between them.

FLESH: AN EARLY FAMILY HISTORY

1. Forgetting

Mother

The first hand coming down from heaven. Her hand.
She hovers above you. It is a premonition
Of life to come, a bird preparing to land.

Your mother's warmth. Her breasts. An impression
Of intensity as softness, and then the bones
Of her knuckles. Cheeks. Neck. The motion

Of her head, swing of her hips. The delicate cones
Of her nipples. The mystery of the navel. Heat.
Cold, Wet. Dry. Milky smells and pheromones.

Where do you begin? With fingers tickling feet
Or lips against skin ? Being lifted high
Then swung to safety? The noises of the street?

Your minor disasters? Hearing your own cry
Echo in your head? There's something lost,
Something buried deep under the eye

You try to see with, something faint as dust
Settled inside your lungs, a history
Tucked in the folds of your body like a cast.

The radio mumbles. A bell rings suddenly.
Light moving across the floor, over the ceiling.
The bird rustles. Her hair. The branches of a tree

Against the window knocking and squealing.

Sleigh Ride

You know the feeling but can't put a name to it.
All beginnings are the same and all are forgotten.
Forgetting is what you've done. You can't undo it

Now or ever. It is the cast you put on
Inside you. You have wandered about her body
All your life, are aware of it as the hidden pattern

You follow. It is as if your life were a parody
Of something she once told you. You taste her skin
First thing in the morning. It is a heady

Delicate babyish smell you must have breathed in
At the outset, when you started forgetting.
Her hands. The bird hovering. Later, a thin

Wrinkled integument with the sun setting
Inside it. Time slips away like the toboggan
Your father once pulled for you. You were sitting

With your brother, clutching him, hanging on
To his arm, everything around you white
And blurred, the sky, the trees, everything gone

Or going, slipping dangerously towards night
Where life too is slippery and you must cling
To the moon or whatever is solid. You're right

To forget this, to remember absolutely nothing.

Dead Babies
(after Canetti)

There's absolutely nothing between them. The ape
Nurses her dead child as though it were alive,
Tenderly cradles its inert furry shape

And won't let go. It's the first imperative
And must be obeyed. She examines eyes
Mouth, nose and ears, attempts to give

Her baby the breast. She grooms it. Tries
To pick it clean. After a week or so
She leaves off feeding but swats at the flies

That settle on its body and continues to show
Deep interest in its cleanliness. Eventually
She begins to set it down, learns to let go.

It starts to mummify and grows horribly smelly.
Now and then she'll bite at the skin until
A limb drops off, then another. Gradually

It decomposes. Even the skin starts to shrivel.
At last she understands at the back of her head.
She plays with furry objects. There is a subtle

Readjustment. Reverse the roles of the dead.
Turn back the clock. Forgetting is good.
You turn and turn within your tiny bed

Until the back of your mind has understood.

The Phantom of the Opera

Things gather in the back of the mind. You find them
Changed yet familiar, everything is in pieces.
Your furry toys, your games: the harmless phantom

Of childish operas is stalking the premises.
You have little idea of the world outside. The wall
Is the limits of language, beyond that the crisis

Of imagination, smashed glass, a noisy hall
Full of children you've never seen, the air
Frozen in attitudes, all too forgettable.

You push your way through the door, down the stair
To a melancholy traffic of cars and the old
Who possess the world and seem to be everywhere.

You push away from your mother but fear the cold
And retreat. She accepts you back with a fury.
She grooms you. Washes you. You are controlled

By her attentions, preserved from injury,
From infection, from your own body, lost
In her larger moods, enduring the battery

Of her breasts and never count the cost.
Your limbs are dropping off. Something dies
As you grow, decay and forget the most

Annoying, ridiculous things. Forgetting is wise.

Outside

You forget so much. Memory drops away,
its phantom limb still waggling. Wipe the slate
clean each time, scrub like there's no yesterday.

Your mother moves off with her innate
Disturbing odours. You run across the floor
And hide in her lap, aware of your own weight.

Outside are executions, show trials. The door
Opens on the operations of the body politic.
There are crowds in the street who want more

Than you can give. There's a school. There's a stick
And a carrot. A boy in a track suit weeps snot
Into his cut sleeve and feels faintly sick

While, in between, the land that time forgot
Is blossoming into enormous flowers,
Great fields you pass in the bus on a hot

Summer afternoon, the smell of ripe hours
Blowsing into poppies, corn and dark blue
Cherries, the sound of a dozen lawnmowers

In a London suburb, pastures passed through,
Wiped clean and rewritten, fields without number
Or name, like a foreign place you never knew,

The smell of flesh you cannot quite remember.

ECLOGUE: HOSPITAL SCENE

A

In the green and white light of the hospital she sat beside him
Just as her parents had sat by her own bedside.
Life was so thin and ragged it hardly seemed possible
To hold it. More than once it had slipped through her fingers
And she had to leap after the trailing string, a faint wisp of cotton,
And make herself light, almost skeletal, so it would support her.

B

The child was her first and he seemed to be slipping beyond her
Into the murk of the past that had got by without him,
Where the pale green was darker, muddier, cloacal,
A wholly internal affair like the lining of memory,
A visceral padding of flesh to block out the image
Of the war that had only quite recently ended.

A

In the green and white light of the hospital they were huddled
          together
Like figures in paintings of sick-beds, with much the same knowledge
That not far away in the meadow bodies were buried,
Where potato and cabbage, maize and huge sunflower
Toiled to the ticking of nature and wrapped the dry bones
In the only available form of inadequate healing.

B

And so they sat without hope or expectation
While trams came and went, and the newspapers carried
The speeches of those in authority, statistics of production,
And ghostly doctors and nurses moved through the ward
Like moths invading a larder, like leaves on the river,
Like almost anything else given to drifting.

2. First Things First

Piano

It's a baby grand with unexceptionable teeth
And a butterfly wing caught in the net curtain.
When touched it answers gently as a breath

Of cold wind, a sensualist in a puritan
Country. It is a hybrid creature with only
Three legs and a faint ephemeral grin,

With feminine curves, a gorgeous womanly
Voluptuousness. It seems almost indecent
To be sitting beneath her, guilty and lonely,

Ignorant of the role she will play. The crescent
Of her one hip is a shelter and the gloss
Of her body temptation. Concupiscent

Discords swell into proper fifths, zealous
Arpeggios clamber over her. Learning
Her vast bourgeois temperament is the cross

A child must bear as she stands burning
In the summer sun. And Chopin and Bartok
Can be enticed from her with their strut and yearning.

You must woo her carefully with wealth and work,
Until one day, like the butterfly she is,
She shrugs and vanishes into the sudden dark

Of history and other shady business.

Stove

The incinerated history of the block
Is trapped within these terracotta stoves
Grumbling and wheezing like a carriage clock

Or faintly glowing like upended loaves.
In winter our great aunts, the elderly,
Huddle beside them in fingerless gloves

Grow older, more transparent, tenderly
Beckoning us to join them. The stove sweats
And sighs with the wind in the frozen northerly

Forests we read about where dogs and cats
Are children in disguise. Life goes up in flames,
The familiar is swept under magic carpets.

Their gingerbread-brown is focus for our games.
We creep up on each other. We touch the tiles
With drops of water that glitter like tiny gems

Sizzling into silence. The stove's mouth smiles
Through its black grille. It could possibly teach
Us something, but what? Downstairs, the piles

Of logs, coal-heaps, old jam-jars, the dark niche
Of the cellar with its guttered candles. We learn
its sunken topography, its slow muttering speech

and bring our rusty buckets with stuff to burn.

Swing

Tenderly they attached the rings to the lintel
Of the door and set the swing into motion
With the child firmly in it. They were gentle

As they pushed, with proper parental caution.
The child's eyes widened. He giggled, kicking his heels
And swallowed the air of the flat like a dizzy potion.

Pendulum-wise it swung to his appeals,
Defying gravity, almost subversive:
The rings rubbed with small metallic squeals.

It was as if the whole world had turned cursive,
Leaning beyond the perpendicular
Into another edgy dimension, massive

And terrifying. His parents stood rectangular,
Respectable, as they would always stand
But ever more blurred, losing shape and colour.

Perhaps this was what they had always planned.
The swing could be hooked up out of the way
When not in use. Only an adult hand

Could take it down and make the whole flat sway.
Mother and father were gods of limited space.
Only they could willingly fade away

Like the child's own faintly breathed-on, mirrored face.

A Lead Soldier

The soldier was the first thing he could weigh
In his closed palm and feel somehow assured.
He watched it as it watched him where he lay,

Knowing he might endure what it endured.
Being a child he was aware of childhood,
Knowing the cell in which he was immured

And all the rules of being bad and good.
His nails ran round the soldier's form, the face,
The back of the knee, the plinth on which it stood

Ready to venture, glaring at a space
Behind the wardrobe or the enemy
Propped by the inkpot, where it had the grace

A child lacks, having no autonomy.
Even inside its box along with others
It held its posture with economy.

It was like having regiments of brothers
Each more valiant than the last, a palette
Of reds and blues. The child was light as feathers,

Too vulnerable. He needed an amulet
To see him through the nights his parents fought.
The soldier was the rough weight of a bullet,

A boiled-down heart, like his, more finely wrought.

Book

There is a graveyard, full moon, and, asleep,
A hero figure. Then, at midnight, ghosts
In their thousands who are doomed to keep

Appointments with the wide awake. Vast hosts
Of them whoo–whoo and helter-skelter, chill
Electric slivers of life at their last posts.

This is a story. Tell me another, until
The stories are exhausted and the dead
Retire to their grave bedrooms in the hill.

The book closes on the double spread
Of the night sky which flows for ever, immense
Beyond the page, lighting stars in the head.

A ghost fades until it is merely presence,
An aura of light-bulbs, curtains, wagging tongues
Speaking a coded semi-conscious sense.

Wake when you can. Children are singing songs
In the playground. Teacher is telling a tale.
The books lie open like a pair of lungs

Breathing words. Ghosts in the graveyard wail
To other moons. The stars have moved so far
Beyond the page they've gone right off the scale,

Small crumbs of icing in an empty jar.

ECLOGUE: FAIR DAY

A

Fair day in Budapest. Little fringed trumpets of cardboard
With barber's-pole patterns. And the man in the trilby
Is down on his haunches with his small son beside him.
It is spring in the park, too early in the century,
In these parts at least, for a snarl up of motorised traffic.
It is legs all the way, a foot-bound Futurist manifesto.

B

Too early for a child to attempt a distinction
Between joy and mere chaos and something of terror.
The largeness of things is an ongoing factor
In the tiny managerial office of his senses
Which registers hands, like his father's, those very same hands,
As the weight of a lonely order of planets.

A

Fair day in Budapest, now tucked into history
In the way you slip a bus-ticket into a book
Or it may be a postcard, or a strip from a serviette
In any case temporary and sure to fall out
When the volume is opened, as it has been, and often.
It is, after all, only a child and his felt-hatted father.

B

Everything slips from the books you are reading:
The plot, the descriptions, the fascinating characters,
And the only thing left is the smell of the pages
Or the way they turned over, and the child that once turned them,
Who slips from the book now. Look, look at him slipping,
And the hand on his shoulder, a moon with its planet.

3. Secret Languages

The Sound of the Radio

Once there were brothers tucked up nice and tight
Inside the world. Cradle, playpen and pram
Littered their double room and broke the night

With streaks of light under the door, the jamb,
The curtain, and the faintly fragile shape
Of crying like the bleating of a lamb.

One was much smaller, little hairless ape
That clung to mother, animal not child,
With eyes, fingers, mouth, everywhere agape,

Seizing just what it could, unreconciled,
Unlike the elder, to the world of the possible,
Its smelly paraphernalia piled

On a painted chest of drawers by the table,
With parents parked in the next room,
Their talk a low buzz fizzing into trouble.

But when it cried one of them would come
Immediately, alert, moving softly but fast
Between furniture, through great bundles of gloom,

The radio suddenly louder, like the ghost
Voice of an enormous world, a slab
Suddenly broad and brilliant as gold-dust

Bringing into their darkness the gift of the gab.

Early Music

The little one was a slow speaker. Not until
The toy violin fell on his head did he mutter
The word 'violin' like a minor miracle.

Language opened its doors to him. He would utter
Prophecies and curses in the vocabulary of music.
Music ran through his fingers like melted butter.

Music would be the saving of him, music or magic.
Life would exercise him no more than those quaint
Ornaments he mastered, the beginner's trick

Of sounding like genius. Women would faint
To hear him, he was so beautiful to see,
And practised night and day without complaint.

Romantic reveries nurtured the folly
Of his parents. Monstrous hopes sat on the stairs
Frowning darkly at the happy family,

(Who were they to give themselves such airs?)
But music was aspiration, they could not breathe without it.
It was the flowering of their sad affairs.

The dead, undoubtedly, were firmly behind it,
Their bloodied faces and emaciated bodies
Resounding through the child, endlessly implicit,

In scales, arpeggios and those awkward studies.

Cleaner

The daily swore like a trooper, but cleaned and cooked
While the parents worked elsewhere, back in the age
Of Uncle Joe Stalin. She was how things looked

In the early fifties. She occupied centre-stage
With her loose tongue and they acted horrified
When the children erupted in foul language.

It was comical. Grandmother would have died
To hear it, being a respectable working class
Woman, who ran to a little sewing on the side,

And as for grandfather, he was dead, alas,
The socialist playwright of the shop-floor
Swept off to Auschwitz in a cloud of gas.

Small rough hands, she had, and a pinafore.
Her nose was snub, her teeth yellow and black
With cigarettes. She would lie down and snore

On the sofa most afternoons, flat on her back,
Then give them a cuddle and some kind of sweet,
And all the rooms were clean as if by magic.

She taught them *fuck* and *fart*, their mouths replete
With her tongue and her bad teeth in their heads,
Then disappeared back down into the street,

Their bodies tucked like small flames in their beds.

Newspaper

The newspaper was faint type on pale grey,
Dissolving into dots on close inspection
As if the whole world could be blown away

Like specks of dust or flimsy bits of fiction.
The place outside was faceless. Words like ranks
Of shadows thinned to an official diction

They learned by osmosis, phalanx by long phalanx,
Until they filled you out and blocked your eyes.
Meanwhile the powdery images of tanks

And flags involved in endless exercise
Expanded over drawers and kitchen shelves
To serve as camouflage for household flies.

Mysterious as blown-out radio-valves,
The children scanned them, seeking to discover
An order of things far beyond themselves,

Another world as vast as the grey river
That ran through everything they ever knew.
They watched the delicate paper lift and quiver

In the draught. And everywhere words blew
And settled. On their skin, on their clothes. The air
Was tiny photographic dots that flew

Straight at their faces, tugging at their hair.

The Pipes

Having been born into an age of pipes
We knew integrity by its sour smell.
Our parent's friends were intellectual types

Who drew and sucked like imperturbable
Monoliths, in their dachas by the lake,
And tapped their sepia fingers on the table

Occasionally producing a dark flake
Of tobacco from their spittled lips. They rocked
In cane chairs set on porches, half-awake,

While in the darkness the clock ticked and tocked
And water gently slopped among the reeds.
Their silences were too grave to be shocked

By wars or arguments or infantile misdeeds.
The village dogs slunk by. They puffed and spat
Like monuments with barely human needs.

Tall wreaths of smoke The curious furry hat
Of adulthood, contentment, stillness. We
Respected their silence. Their empty, flat

Voices. Their deaths would be ours eventually.
We would light their pipes, enter their myths.
When the clock stopped ticking we too would be free

To turn ourselves into such monoliths.

ECLOGUE: AT THE STATION

A

It is November and snowing, like something out of Tolstoy,
Here at the railway station where a woman wearing a muff
Is waiting on the platform, while thousands of faces
Swim in and out of focus with suitcases and bundles
In a fug of anxiety that rises from their mouths
And blots out their features one breathtaking moment.

B

Here stride the soldiers with peaked caps, rifles and kitbags
That belong to a popular movie, so fiction and cinema
Seem to have entered the world, or shifted abruptly
Into the realm of the real, which has blossomed in capital letters,
Into Death, Execution, Resistance, Night Raid, and Crackdown,
All on display at the station, glamorous, vigilant.

A

It is November and snowing, much as it always does
In films of November. Families with children
Are huddled on benches, learning their lines just in case
Of Night Raid or Crackdown. The city is muttering
Into its threadbare, capacious but wholly inadequate sleeve
Its mutterings carried down platforms and carriages.

B

The soldiers are watching the woman who stands very straight
Mysterious as Garbo but infinitely dustier
As the train with its vast preoccupations draws nearer
And the film rolls on with the scene of her jumping
In front of the engine, just as we're all of us jumping
Into a film of snow, on a screen, as she coils, uncoils and jumps.

4. Her Adult Occupations

When she leaned over the light-box

When she leaned over the light-box her face shone
As though she herself had been the source of light,
A moon to a diffused rectangular sun.

Transparent bands of film flopped in tight
Orthodox curls over the edge of it,
And her hair too fell forward, black as night.

Her hands made nervous movements, delicate,
Bird-like, calculated, unerringly precise,
Her head swaying, a harshly under-lit

Mask that caricatured the familiar face.
Whatever it was she was giving herself to
Demanded close attention. The edifice

Of her presence multiplied and grew
In shadows on the wall and the dark hair
Swung to and fro. Meanwhile, her fingers drew

The shadows of light images from the air
Till the tension told on her back and wrists and eyes
And she sat up straight, as if whatever prayer

She'd been engaged on was over. The brush lies
On the table. The film curls on the floor.
The light in the box dazzles. No one dies

In photographs. Then she bends down once more.

Her knees drawn together

Her knees drawn together under the table, she wears
A pair of man's trousers and has pencilled on
A moustache. The elder of two children stares

At her, disorientated. Her voice has gone,
To be replaced by something deeper: a gruff
Stranger's on an official commission.

If this is a joke it isn't quite enough
To make them laugh or simply play along
But there is no way they can call her bluff.

Their father, engaged in talk, sees nothing wrong,
And frowns as if considering a question
She has raised. The world to which they belong

Is beyond speculation or suggestion,
Two grown-up dolls moving on a stage
In danger of spontaneous combustion.

He stands up. She rises. It takes an age.
The giants evoke a slow music of basses
And tubas. The terrible badinage

Between them comes to an end. Their faces
Burn with suppressed laughter as she wipes
Away the moustache. His finger traces

Her light skin between the smudged stripes.

Despite the heavy snow she is almost skipping

Despite the heavy snow she is almost skipping
Down the moonlit street. The children clutch
Their parents' hands. High up, eaves are dripping

Icicles. No cars. No people. Not very much
Of anything at this time. Silence. It is two
In the morning in the New Year. They watch

Their mother in amazement. She floats through
The city in their heads, an apparition
Of adult high spirits, like a wholly new

Secret. The winter is exotic, White Russian
In its dense pallour and unheard-of chill.
Minus twenty-five. They sense the passion

In her pleasure, as they did at the high table
In the feasting hall with its pig's head. Never before
Have they been up so late. They know they are still

Children, and that she's immeasurably more
Than they can understand. Their father moves
Cautiously beside her, testing the slippery floor

On her behalf. A hard gust of wind shoves
Them forward as they pass unfamiliar blocks
On strange corners with their furry leather gloves,

Their fancy trousers tucked into thick socks.

Something breathless, frighteningly urgent

Something breathless, frighteningly urgent,
Seemed to be batting around her when she fluffed
Her hair out gypsy-fashion, her mouth pungent

With garlic cloves, indelicately stuffed
With bread and dripping. She drew her eyebrows thick
In high black arches to match the rounded tuft

Of her black beauty spot. Her scarlet lipstick
Was dangerous as blood and not maternal.
This transformation was an adult trick

To scare the world out of its eternal
Terrors, and us into strangeness. She would flirt
With hard-faced men: the fat KGB colonel

In the office, informers who dished dirt.
Such representatives of outer dark
Would all be cowed with a flick of her wide skirt.

And we too would be cowed, as if the stark
Facts of existence had sharpened in our eyes
And hovered there like an ambiguous mark –

Much like the beauty spot in fact, the cries
Of distant bedrooms, the doings of stray dogs,
The deep unsettling realm of adult lies,

A sense of oil and wheels and endless cogs.

With nails filed smooth into deep curves

With nails filed smooth into deep curves and points
(Her hands had modelled jewellery in a store)
She bent her fingers back against the joints

And though the boys would plead with her: no more!
She knew these were electric attributes
To hold them still or lift them from the floor.

The body can do so much: bellows and flutes
Through which you blow, or weapons you may wield
To good effect. You wear it as it suits

And walk about in it with your eyes peeled,
But cannot see through what remains opaque
Or penetrate behind its foreign shield.

Her fingers curled into their hearts. The ache
Had found a home where it might live
Forever if her fingers did not break,

And even then the nails would surely drive
Deeper until they could not tell them from
The fabric of their beings which would thrive

On such acute discomfort. So fingers drum
On tables and the eyes open at night,
And small electric pulses lift and thrum

Through bones and lodge there like an ammonite.

ECLOGUE: MIRROR

A

Mirror into which we continually disappear. Those eyes
Are not ours, nor have they ever been, the more they have looked
For that other, the missing one. She was putting on make-up
And I was behind her, and sun on the wall was aching to speak
But all it could say was goodbye, and again, and goodbye.
And that was the best of it, the joy of the catch in the throat.

B

I saw you behind me and knew you were watching. We hung
In the air like shadows with bodies, and time was just leaving, going
Out of the door, into the dark of the hall where the coats hang.
I put on my coat and went out. There was shopping to do and
        the street
Extended itself in a version of central perspective.
Life was geometry, a drawing of lines with an architect's pencil.

A

Mirror into which so much has disappeared. Shop-windows
Staring back at the traffic, photographs in the album
Of lost things, almost an X-ray of bones buried under the pavement.
I was watching her go. It was foggy, my glasses had misted.
There were grease marks all over the lens as she turned the next
        corner
Facing the sun now, directly. She was burning to ashes.

B

You are always behind me. I am washing my hands at the basin.
I stand and imagine you shaving, your face is pushed forward
Practically touching the mirror. I hear the noise of the shaver.
An aeroplane broods in the distance above the high cloud. I hear you
Saying I love you, and watch myself move from the frame of the
        mirror
Into the space of the room, which is empty and burning.

5. My Fathers

My fathers, coming and going

Moustaches and grey homburgs: our fathers were
Defined by properties acquired by chance –
Or by divine decree. Standing behind her

In rooms, on stairs, figures of elegance,
They came and went in a murmur of soft voices,
Objects of bewilderment and romance.

How many of them on the premises?
Some worked twelve hours a day in an office
In the city, some placed bristly kisses

On our brows, some would simply embarrass
Us for no particular reason. Their age
Was indeterminate. They would promise

Anything befitting their patronage.
Were all these fathers one? And was it you,
My father, who pushed me in that carriage

I can't remember now before time flew
And took her away as it will take us all?
I feel myself flying. It's like passing through

Clouds in an aeroplane in its own bubble
Of air, a slightly bumpy ride down
Towards a runway as we rise and fall

Above the brilliant lights of a big town.

Their histories and fabled occupations

The histories and fabled occupations
Of their fathers lay somewhere off the map
In provinces lost to their imaginations.

The knowledge they had was fed to them scrap by scrap
And was all they ever needed. The fathers' presence
Was sufficient. They watched them through a gap

In their mother's eyes, beyond the fence
Of reason, arriving wreathed in smells of their own,
Some reassuring, others wild and tense

With dangers they had carried home from town.
Their fathers were the seas they read about
But never saw, in which a child could drown

However he might wave his arms and shout
For help. A singular compound figure stood
On the threshold of their bodies and looked out.

Mysterious rodents emerged from the wood
And scurried up the stairs at night to nibble
At their faces. They woke covered in blood.

Their father's moustache was a scary scribble
Above a friendly voice. His kindness shook
The world out of its endless incomprehensible

Rigor mortis like the closing of a book.

My father, crawling across the floor

He crawls across the floor. His dangling tie
Distracts the child. He hauls the child in the air
And swings it round, once, twice. He holds it high

Above his head. In the forest, a bear
Lurches towards the cabin. Almost night.
Goldilocks sits in the deepest chair

By the table working up an appetite.
Time starts up, judders and stops again
Its flooded engine refusing to ignite.

We're conked out here, stuck in the slow lane
Of history, where my father comes home late
From work as always and will not complain.

Seventy-two hours he labours for the state
Weekdays, Saturdays, doing what, why, how,
We do not ask him, but accept his fate.

Time is forever in an endless Now
Except in dreams, anxieties, and school,
Though time ticks over far behind his brow

According to a superimposed rule
We touch when we touch him. We hear him roar
In distant forests where his masters drool

And lumber playfully across the floor.

My father carries me across a field

My father carries me across a field.
It's night and there are trenches filled with snow.
Thick mud. We're careful to remain concealed

From something frightening I don't yet know.
And then I walk and there is space between
The four of us. We go where we have to go.

Did I dream it all, this ghostly scene,
The hundred-acre wood where the owl blinked
And the ass spoke? Where I am cosy and clean

In bed, but we are floating, our arms linked
Over the landscape? My father moves ahead
Of me, like some strange, almost extinct

Species, and I follow him in dread
Across the field towards my own extinction.
Spirits everywhere are drifting over blasted

Terrain. The winter cold makes no distinction
Between them and us. My father looks round
And smiles then turns away. We have no function

In this place but keep moving, without sound,
Lost figures who leave only a blank page
Behind them, and the dark and frozen ground

They pass across as they might cross a stage.

Like a black bird

Like a black bird against snow, he flapped
Over the path, his overcoat billowing
In the cold wind, as if he had trapped

The whole sky in it. We watched trees swing
Behind him, lurching drunkenly, blurred
Bare twigs and branches, scrawny bits of string,

And as we gazed ahead the snowflakes purred
In our ears, whispering the afternoon
Which grew steadily darker and more furred.

His face was in shadow, but we'd see it soon,
As he approached it slowly gathered shape:
His nose, in profile, was a broken moon,

His hat a soft black hill bound round with tape,
His raised lapels held his enormous eyes
Between them. The winter seemed to drape

Itself about him as if to apologise
For its own fierceness, hoping to grow warm
Through physical contact, and we, likewise,

Ran towards him, against a grainy storm
Of light and damp. It was so long ago
And life was then in quite another form,

When there were blacker days and thicker snow

ECLOGUE: SHOES

A

Innocuous shape in a side street, a plaque by the entrance
With the name of the school written across it,
Nothing important, only the staircase waiting
For the roll-call of children to trample and shuffle
In some kind of order up to a classroom then vanish
Into the books in the stock-room on loose bits of paper.

B

I hear the shrill voices die as the door shuts.
I'm troubled and moved by the prospect of you in your best shoes
Entering and remaining, locked away in there for ever,
My very self splitting as I walk to the city
To where I must work but where something is missing,
The shoes you set off in that I had just polished that morning.

A

Innocuous shape in the side street, the screaking of blackboards,
While downstairs the business of everyday living
Is running itself, and a teacher holds forth on her subject
Which is Time and Behaviour: the way that the world wends
Its passage through time, which even now vanishes
Down a tight passage between sleep and awakening.

B

I hear the shrill voices of Time and Behaviour, the teachers
In thin dusty suits are loudly insistent we hear them,
The shoes that I polished are under a desk and the fingers
I checked for dirt are spread on the desktop. The dead years
Are always available, just open the desklid,
There in the books with their blue paper covers.

THE DREAM HOTEL

The Dream Hotel

As if the sea were entering through the window,
it was that close. Flecks of burning ice thrown
from the rocks it struck, each single fleck blown
sharp-toothed into the house. Meanwhile, below
there were guests waiting to check in, a clerk
to register them, luggage piling at doors.
This was the form of the dream. Polished floors
were swimming in water, a green-grey dark.
From the top of the cliff you could see rain
gathering on the horizon, not yet ready
to fall but on its way. In one room two lips
were joined together, hands resting on hips,
the pair of them increasingly unsteady
as the flood rolled in like an enormous stain.

You wake to a light on the ceiling. How long
have you been awake? You lie next to him,
the one you always lie with. Some vague, dim
recollection. Years of memory. The song
of the sirens. The glow of the clock-radio
is green and gentle. Classical music, faint,
barely audible, oozes from it. Something quaint
about all this, your life passing on its slow
unforgiving way. The shape in the bed stirs
in its sleep, rolls over. You feel the steady swell
rising in you. You hear the sea again.
It is still far off, a slowly approaching train
down a long tunnel that leads to the hotel
and the two lovers, just as his lips touch hers.

The Gods of Tiepolo

1

Sometimes when you look up on a bright day,
the clouds have drawn apart, exposing a blue
that, for a moment, you can almost look through.
You're surveying a stage long after the play
has finished. Above you, Tiepolo
presents a weightless mass of gods and legs
in endless apotheosis, delicate as eggs
in a cup, or naked skin in an afterglow
when legs and arms float off into half-sleep
and breasts settle warmly against the ribcage
slipping vaguely down its slopes, while the flat
lower belly shimmers and fingers keep
curling and uncurling like an open page
in a slight breeze. But you can imagine that.

2

So you imagine it. Although this is
the soft sell version, somewhere beyond which
the world is singing at a sharper pitch,
its shrieks full of glass, crowded with casualties:
men in ridiculous wigs, women with waists
pinched to a tight ring, thin children in beds
with soiled sheets, the poor with their shaved heads
and hollow eyes, cruel sexual gymnasts
one step from madness, new forms of rough trade,
a puritan hell which no amount of light
can keep from sinking deeper into flames.
Imagine it. And through that? The betrayed
clear blue of something very simple, as trite
as touch, the sound of the most common names.

3

You listen to them. It's no different there
next door, next year. The sky is lightly cracking.
An enormous gentleness billows its wing
and you too are up aloft, somewhere in the air
on an internal flight, your safety belt

clipped shut, with a glass of whisky on the rocks
on a swivelling tray, among lazy flocks
of clouds that snuggle up to you then melt,
substantial as any god or human life.
Now you're a god. There's something piercing and sad
about this knowledge, as if there were nothing but
that rococo blue which beggars all belief,
the world below disordered, a ragged, mad
arena of blood which runs and refuses to clot.

4

In this particular Tiepolo,
The Finding of Moses,where a Venetian
beauty, dressed in the height of contemporary fashion,
stands in for the daughter of the Pharaoh,
your eyes discover a female figure, vast
thighed yet slender and long, with cheekbones sleek
as a greyhound and eyes that plead to speak
a mind so powerful it makes your own fly fast.
The even blue sky above her seems to spring
straight from her gaze which comprehends your own.
It solves the world, bandages its wounds,
ties up its severed limbs with blood-soaked string,
walks the streets of explosions up and down,
and smiles at all its terrible, sad sounds.

5

Keep flying, pilot, We're gods of air and fire,
our clay feet stuck in loam. Bring me a drink
and let me watch the clouds move as I think
of something clear as glass in the empire
of the bladed, whose agents are generous.
I'm fed up of this Rococo court, that sits
tremendous arsed, and will shortly be blown to bits
on its mountain-top five-star hotel terrace.
It's dark outside. Soon the movies come on
with hollow icons and interminable chases.
I want a woman of luminous intelligence to heal
my hypochondria. Soon we shall land on the sun
with smooth, unruffled, tanned, innocent faces,
staring at endless blue. It's no big deal.

Naples Yellow

His skin was Naples Yellow. He was wearing a suit
of cinematic glamour as if light dust
had settled on him. He was easy to trust
and spoke with a confidence that was absolute.
'Mon vieux,' he said in French, 'I think that we
are two of a kind. Nothing is what it seems.
Fiction confuses real and imagined dreams
and passes them off as plausibility.
Unfinished books are stacking themselves high
in corners: their characters have breath
but no desire to breathe. Raskolnikov
dies with an axe in his hand, not afraid to die.
Prince Myshkin is slowly walking to his death.
In every book there's someone turning lights off.'

It seemed he knew about unfinished books
but it was like meeting people anywhere,
like the man glimpsed in the café, in the chair,
in a waiting-room.   Sometimes the whole world looks
unfinished like that. The bed is not quite made,
the sun spreads uneasily across the wall,
and the boy over the street is kicking his ball
against the fence in an odd patch of shade...
Somebody's hand snakes out to clutch your own.
It starts to teach you something. You start to write
a sentence but the words escape. You lie
on the bed exhausted, having put the book down
some hours ago. It's the time of night
when minds move sideways out of symmetry.

'As your mind's moving now. The whole thing lists
like a doomed boat. Where are the passengers?
Who would you save from those all too tangible dangers?
Those you knew first, or the escapologists
you met much later? Remember this is fiction
and not life. The laws of the two places
sometimes coincide but different graces

attend on them. Some carry conviction,
others' – and here he snapped his fingers – 'fade
like clothes in sunlight.' He himself looked faint.
The whole café was dreamlike but he knew
that too. 'Take yourself,' he said. Light played
on his white shirt like fingers exploring paint.
'You can't play at both passengers and crew.

You hear yourself talk. Some book has it down
in black and white. And this is not just theoretical,
as you'll prove for yourself. You'll get it all
thrown back at you. And no, you needn't frown
so sceptically...' This monologue might have
continued, gone on for ever, but the voice
had almost died away. It was my choice
to make him vanish. 'You think you'll save
yourself like this?' was the very last thing
he said and smiled. The diner opposite
was positively translucent in the light.
And so I fell asleep. The story was going
as stories do, no need to tinker with it.
My eyes were blind. Whatever was, was right.

Pompeian Red

These are the mysteries and this is the house
of the mysteries. This is the red earth below,
and this is the flower we no longer know
that the woman holds. Here dancers carouse
in spirals acting out something we've long
lost track of. Here is the entrance, the stairs
that lead down into a nether place of affairs
we do not penetrate. Here is the song
they're singing in a strange tonality
which is said to move the spheres. Here is death
in a black gown sprinkled with flames and leaves
you find only under this buried city.
Here is the perfume they wore on their breath.
Here is the fabric the hand twists and weaves.

Here on the other hand is a café
with a glazed terrace. A woman is serving whatever
is there to be served. Downstairs flows the river
of plain plumbing which serves to wash away
things that are washed away. It is the Boulevard
Montparnasse and people are eating omelettes
au jambon and fraises au citron. People forget
what they eat and talk instead. It is hard
to forget this. Easier to remember
than mysteries, though this is also one.
The lava rushes down like busy traffic.
Eyes dance in their orbits, move in their limber
circuits like planets round a distant sun
that beats and pulses under molten brick.

Red suggests lipstick. The entry to a cave
that goes on for ever, a place of changes
and cast shadows. The waiter arranges
cutlery and sets out dishes that deprave
and purify. Persephone glides
down corridors of grass into the heart of Dis
and Paolo and Francesca bend to kiss
over the book they're reading. Each rides

the current that blows him or her, over
omelettes or fraises and a glass of red
house wine, which arrives, circumspect
as the waiter. The glazed panels cover
and reveal at the same time but the dead
keep talking as their thoughts and mouths connect.

Imagine the whole world under glass. The ash
in the ashtray. The dust in the urn. The face
at the bottom of the cup, the empty space
between more emptiness, glass one longs to smash
simply because it's glass. And yet it's lovely,
this sunlight trapped in the purring moment:
nothing will ever be better than the present,
it says, and you believe it as it moves gravely
past you. This is the mystery. This is the house
that guards it. This is the town by the volcano
which is silent as if for ever but not for ever,
the house of omelettes and wine and fraises
where everyone is free to come and go
down concrete steps into the subway river.

In all of this, it is the omelettes, the berries
with a slice of lemon, the most poignant things
that best embody the ritual. Ash clings
to them but they burn on internal batteries
recharging themselves constantly. Perhaps
that's the heart of it, nature, or the word
which stands for nature, that which is interred
with the body yet ticks on when bone snaps
under the slumped weight of earth. The red eye
winking on the dish, footprints on the grass,
the sudden movement of a ghostly head
trapped in the knowledge that it has to die
and glow like this under the terrace glass
with simple berries of Pompeian red.

Purple Passage after Nolde

1

It was how I imagined the sea to be
but it never was, not at least at Margate.
How could it match up that intensity
or resolve itself to such terrible weight
of feeling? Imagine yourself a spiritual squid
spurting ink, or pissing into your pants
at some desolate station (not the squalid
pool at your feet but the release) while your parents
frown into the fog at the back of your head.
Life squirts out at high pressure. Then the drowned
rise up. You see a red headed Christ weep
into his sleeve, consorting with the dead,
and from the sea emerges a faint sound
of relief like a man farting in his sleep.

2

You are sinking into an orchid or a tulip.
Now mother has closed her dreamy eyes
you come round by the side door and slip
inside with bees and multi-coloured flies
into the house of nature as the demon sees it,
a dark disgusting mess and far from Attic.
It's neither ideal, nor clear. You cannot seize it
with your hands. It refuses geometric
imperatives, hangs loose, amorphous, yet
is glorious and opens on dissection
on dark reds and maroons, a distinct strain
of colour like a purple passage set
in classical prose and under its protection
burning away your skin with acid rain.

Romantic Love

It was early November. The grass glowed
under a frame of light. A red bridge crossed
a dual carriageway. The train was lost
between two cities. It was as if it followed
its own chronology forward into time
which sat still watching as it watched birds
and mice, the progress of rust and the words
spoken in each carriage, all with sublime
attention to detail. Not far off but elsewhere
two people were kissing. One's hand moved
on the other's breast. A fistful of blonde hair.
The tail of a shirt. Who else have you loved?
they asked each other. Tell me, was there anyone?
But no one heard them speak. The train moved on.

*

And two girls in the next seat. One said: 'So he
went to the top of the car park and threatened
to throw himself off, but then his friend,
the one who had stolen his lover, felt sorry
and joined him and said he'd jump too, so they
came down and went to a club where there were
lapdancers and got drunk.' But we'd lost her
in the noise. The wind had carried her away.
Their voices continued lapping as at the bank
of a river, wearing it away with their tongues,
dragging along shopping trolleys, brief ranks
of refuse and the words of popular songs,
and we watched them talking excitedly, their eyes
as dazzling as the wings of household flies.

*

The man who had raped the girl at the pool recalled
his wife, how he'd bring her her morning tea
then feel her tits, and they'd fall to it enthusiastically.
That at least was his story. His listeners were appalled.
He clearly missed her although he was a brute
who had probably forced her to have sex
on his own terms. By now she was his ex-
and he'd been alone for years. That was the root
of the problem, an educated man remarked.
He talked of fucking. She referred to it
in other terms. It was her breast and not her tit
he held. Such a man should not have embarked
on a mature relationship. These sorry pricks,
he ventured, are soon hoist by their semantics.

*

They wouldn't let go of each other's hands,
since if they did they might drift apart into
the stream of the universe. And it was true,
they did let go, and there were no real strands
holding them together. But later one
entered the underworld to rescue the other
and they almost made it through, lover to lover.

Two schoolkids were walking home alone
beside the railway line with dark berries
beckoning them and marks where others had lain
among the tussocks with the blood-red stain
on their fingertips, their childhood miseries
gathering dust and weight.

                    Incidentals both.
The flight path of desire. The dazzled moth.

Rough Guide

...*your image destroys*
itself, remakes itself, and is never weary
OCTAVIO PAZ, 'The Prisoner'

Impossible to look directly into
another's eyes. Impossible to look
into your own. You read the dense book
of being like a document you flick through.

Eyes, even an inch apart, are blurs,
clouds, like the concept of yesterday
which has an entity you sometimes stray
into beyond the limits of his and hers.

The unknown: the roughest of the rough guides,
and all it says is: you're here, you'd better make
the best of it. You entered by mistake
and so you'll leave. It's what the route map hides

and languages obscure, the magnetic pull
of all you ever see of the beautiful.

*

But I have seen the beautiful. I know
its contours and the rough guide it provides
is blissfully specific: the hand that rides
the ridge of the collarbone or moves along the brow,

the perfect form of momentary light
in this line or another. It's what Blake
saw at the top of the stair, the terrible earthquake
at the root of the flesh we think of as delight.

It's what you see when you shut your eyes and see,
the angel with the whip or a flaming sword
that burns your eyes down to the spinal cord,
the shit, blood, semen smell of mortality

you get used to because it follows you
everywhere and is both beautiful and true.

Silver Age

Rain so silver you can reach out and grasp
whole clear rods of it, and when it shatters
on the pavement it turns into a clasp
or a ring or dripping necklace that flatters
the neck of the cold queen who wears it beneath
her stately head, or so you imagine
in your childish sleep while watching your breath
sparkle and condense at the fine margin
of a legend which involves the moon,
a hero on a white horse down a lane
at midnight by the graveyard and a girl
glimmering gently like a pool or pearl
who will appear at his cold side as soon
as day breaks to the sound of winter rain.

When day breaks to the sound of winter rain
the curtains open and the legend fades
to clocks and traffic. Now the old refrain
of tick and shrug, the shops in the arcades,
the road to school, and that stranger, the queen
transmogrified into a schoolmistress.
Now pools in potholes, the viridian green,
of playing fields, corridors and emptiness.
Now a thin slice of silver at the pane
of glass above the putty and a low
mass of cloud dragging the window through
a dark infusion of thunder-bloated blue
which gathers towards December snow,
with moonlight locked into a drop of rain.

The moonlight locked inside a drop of rain
runs down the window. The hero on the horse
follows a mysterious predestined course
to school. Down by the cuttings a slow train
breathes steam across its own glittering face
before vanishing down the tunnel ahead.
The schoolmistress is getting into bed.
The graveyard mumbles in its sleep. The space
between lamp-posts grows darker and more lost.

The rails in the cuttings deepen into silver.
All images and nothing more. The ghost
of Christmas Past enters, raddled in lace,
bringing in Time gift-wrapped on a salver,
like a gesture of contrition for bad grace.

Time is where things get born. The silver salver
is the moon dressed as a handy metaphor,
an aristocratic prop and nothing more,
the moon's a prop for something else that's silver,
and so on down to the empty-handed butler.
Love, when I was a child, I thought like a child
and left out my shoes for the man who piled
up presents like a perfect daddy, none subtler
in his approaches, coming only when
I was asleep. And his bounty was infinite:
he had to lever his gifts in with a shoe-horn
(my socks peeked out, like something being born).
And so time passed, down to the very minute
I write these thoughts down with my adult pen.

Terre Verte

1

The things that grow out of earth! Weird, stunted
knobbly things with hair or other roughnesses,
priapic little gods, gods patched from dresses
the doll once wore, some knuckled, some blunted
by their emergence from the medium
that nourished them. Roots, tubers, the carrot
like a raw joke, all that wood spirit,
earth under nails, in folds of skin, at the eardrum:
Van Gogh's Potato Eaters, Brueghel's peasant
belching into a corner, calloused feet
banging on a dirt floor to a harsh pipe,
the stumpy-digit, heavy-brow, big-earlobe type.
They come with flowers to rooms suddenly neat
and scented, refreshing and distinctly pleasant.

Shall I play Priapus with you? Shall we find
the old shed with its smelly newspapers,
dead mice and dried grass? Shall we cut capers
among onion sacks, rolling on a fat behind?
Shall we cut the crap instead? Shall we get
down to it, the deed of darkness, the two
of us? Tell me what you'd like me to do?
Shall I play finial to your crocket?
Needle to your haystack? Camel to eye
of needle, pig to trough, horse to water,
nose to grindstone with a yo-ho-ho
and a bottle of something on which to grow
merrier still? Will you play Green Man's daughter
to the fat hog in his reeky hormonal sty?

2

Consider the texture of *terre verte*,
how it filters underneath the skin:
flesh tint is drawn across it into thin
cold layers of dew intended to subvert
the whole arrangement by a kind of pun.
It's beautiful to touch, is like a dream
of water eating away the bed of the stream
it flows through, leaving nothing for anyone.
Its lovely drowned face materialises
for one moment only under green fronds
between the bars of a supermarket trolley,
then goes off underground, down an alley
you can't enter, and surfaces in ponds
from which a stagnant round aroma rises.

The traveller in his shaggy coat: he
has it bad. And that one there with his rocking
laptop: I wouldn't trust him. The panicking
baby-boomer with his bald patch and anxiety.
They're only after one thing, all of them.
The look in their eyes tells you they're somewhere
at the edge of a joke life failed to prepare
them for, at the withered end of the stem
that leads back into earth and is terrifying.
What wouldn't they do for one moment of grace,
one leaf curling back, brash petals extent
and soft at the heart of an awaited event,
for one beautiful drowned forgiving face
to watch them in their sleep and through their dying.

Turquoise

1

Good to have reached the turquoise age. Not green
not blue but something in between, this
smoky, crystalline concentration, clean
as an iceberg, astringent as the kiss
of water on iron. So your hair drifts
across the sky where everything turns grey.
So the louring cloud-mass shifts
and colour filters into day.
So, between folds of skin your sea-grey eyes
echo the green of your jumper which is turquoise.
(Wings of house flies or dragonflies or butterflies
hover briefly, freeze into flightless poise.)
Perhaps we've chosen this very spot, this now,
and might return if only we knew how.

2

The balance is tipping. We feel the scales
go down. We live in a fortunate age.
Our teeth are still our own, our tops and tails
are in order. We need not rage
against the dying of the light. We touch
each other's skin with pleasure and trace
the lines of limbs, squeezing neither too much
nor too little. The fine bones of the face
retain a sort of tender brittleness,
their threatened beauty yields a thrill
as fingers follow eyelids or caress
the whorls of the ear with acquired skill.
But still the scales go down. Under the dress,
under the shirt and vest, it's all downhill.

3

We watch a TV documentary
on breasts, It's so bloody American,
so pathetically anxious to carry
its terrors like trophies. One thin old woman
grimaces and waves, performs a burlesque.
Her pathos has turned comic. When we laugh
it's not quite at her. Something in the mask
parodies us, part sassy and part naff,
making uneasiness easy. In the dark
my hand slides across your thigh. I sink
my teeth into your neck. Your fingernails spark.
Electrical appliances go on the blink.
Even this gentle pressure leaves a mark,
a turquoise, purple, blackening smear of ink.

4

Our knees are stiff, getting up is a pain.
We take care of our bowels, eat sensibly,
nothing too spicy after nine. No gain
in weight. No dope. No fags. I calmly drain
my glass of Jameson's but feel my heart
accelerate. Sheets full of cancer haunt
the chest of drawers. Minor discomforts start
long trains of thought. The mirror's gaunt
reflection follows us about the room.
Skulls in the desert open their dry mouths
to utter comic prophecies of doom.
They're desperate to confront us with home truths.
You'll turn to prose, fools! We reply in mime,
watching our shadows coupling. There's still time.

5

Turquoise. Under the sea, in slim leaves
of current the fish are brilliant repulsive
flecks of light. The predator deceives
its prey by simulating softness, gives
only to swallow. Sharp, spiny exoskeletons
form ridges to scrape a knee on. A squid
lounges, hunched and expectant. Patterns
of weed on rock form an undulating grid.
I watch my skin grow ridges. Some organic
process throws up warts, disfigurements.
Fronds of grey at the temple. Hair less thick
than it once was. We observe events
like divers in an alien ocean. But then
oceans are (it is their nature) alien.

6

Turquoise. It was an old woman's parasol
lying in the waiting room. Under its wings
the trapped air of the decade. Chirrupings
of dead birds. The half-dressed discarded doll
in the garage. I've seen one queuing up
at the post office counter, rubbing her hands
beside garish coloured advertising stands,
her complexion delicate as a chipped cup.
This poem's becoming elegiac, like her.
In Viennese cafés the waiters hum
whole operettas into aged ears. The words come
naturally, settling on a line of fur,
between the fingers of gloves. Time to kill
between the opening parasol and the bill.

7

Try turquoise once more. Turkish opulence.
Think of those soft cushions and the bleak curve
of the scimitar. The pasha's residence
is where we used to live. The girls would serve
sticky confections as we lay in bed
watching light crumple across the ceiling rose.
The petals were stirring overhead,
the leaves of the window would open and close
and air would billow through. Occasionally
we'd hear the whine of an ambulance, wake
to boys on motorbikes with their crude reveille.
Sometimes the bed itself would gently shake
beneath us. Of course this was years ago,
or never happened. It's getting hard to know.

8

Hermione, the teacher of Greek grammar,
has her face reconstructed by computer
animation. This lends a touch of glamour
to her more prosaic status as a tutor.
('A studious and meek schoolmistress
without a trace of show or ornament,'
said Petrie, another scholar.) Her tenderness
has a stern edge, that is true, but her scent
is deeply sensuous and grave, her hair
parted in the middle shows a light line
of lovely mortal skin, perfectly aware
of its mortality as part of the design.
She emerges from the photo-booth and waits
for the line of four to slip out through the gates.

9

Death is more Woody Allen than Lord Byron.
Being there at the time is the only drag.
No one gives us a branch to hang our spare tyre on
or offers to hide our face in a paper bag.
It's a bit of a joke, this old curmudgeon drone
and sneer. A Larkinesque panicky shrug.
So Mary Magdalene turns into a crone,
and Balzac to an energetic slug.
A true Lawrentian ripeness is the goal,
but somehow the body gets so out of breath
it loses contact with the panting soul
and fails to make the seasonal Ship of Death.
And all that violet eye, and turquoise gaze
drowns in a murky swirling sea of days.

10

The Shakespearian ending which turns round
to claim your immortality in words
performs a gesture. I like its human sound
and proud disdain. I like its afterwards
and quibbles, its hyperboles, its dumb
struggle with silence. And after all, there's truth
in its assertions. How many have come
to the sonnets, from the pimply youth
with his 'A' Levels, to the old botanist
dying on his sofa, mouthing the lines?
I cannot myself close a perfect fist
about the couplet which defines
the perfect closure, capturing desire.
I too am burning in the turquoise fire.

Venice

Because there's nothing that will last for ever
except perhaps ideas, I think of cities:
Vicenza, Verona, Venice, clarities
enduring for a while beside some river
rolling through them, or a crisp sour sea
lapping their feet, lost in a freezing fog,
exquisite in the ice. Something might jog
your memory of them, or any memory,

because memory too is an idea: you think
rationally but you feel your thoughts,
and watch them rise, Byzantine, in a square
heavy with cupolas whose breasts are bare
ideas of breasts that no idea supports,
canals, black water, waking dreams, rough drink.

The Breasts

She gathered up her breasts in her two hands
like small explosions, a soft outward flow,
a timing device that anytime could blow.
So life hangs on the slenderest of strands,
a lover's hunger can seem all of it,
a child, an image in the mirror, hope,
the way a back, or pair of hips might slope,
or how two closing bodies click and fit.

Time is always against us. Youth slips down
the polished shoulder like a loosening strap.
She looked down from her bosom to her lap
and ran her palms over her dressing gown,
her mirrored face drowned in a cloud of dust:
How beautiful, she thought, and how unjust.

Comical Roses in a Cubic Vase

1

There are people who grow wobbly at the knees
at the touch or scent of flowers, botanists
turned erotomanes, foiled aesthetes with spots
and bad breath, beautiful women seeking
analogies for themselves which might explain
their own bold beauty, people driven mad
or just a little queer by anything petal-clad.

Myself, I loved the way the roses could squeeze
up against each other, like a crowd of accordionists
at an impromptu party in an old-fashioned telephone-box.
I loved their funny riotous colours leaking
into the air, lost in an invisible rain
of atoms of which I was a part, the way their fall
could elicit from me something tight-furled, personal.

2

Something about the stark voluptuous thrust
of the flowerheads opening their mouths wide,
makes me think of the pores of my own skin,
and of every human orifice that allows
the world access, billowing with colour,
Alizarin Crimson perhaps, and creamy white,
like a Tennysonian chorus, dark and bright,

all with the faintest coat of luminous dust
in the light of the window, and the garden outside
yearning for access to the garden within;
outside, where there is a certain bending of boughs
and the whole earth is like a deep damp cellar,
and inside, with its carpets, tables and chairs,
and short-lived plant forms covered in fine hairs.

3

A pheasant billowed through the cemetery,
its colours exquisite but with a comical look on its face
in the blank red napkin where its eyes were situated,
and rabbits in tens panicked in small white dots
shooting over the edge, down to the railway cuttings.
It was a glorious late afternoon. The children slept
in their graves while the wonderful pheasant stepped

delicately through their dangerous territory
and everything was busily seeking its place.
Even the roses in the glass cube stated
some kind of claim, like the rabbit scuts,
to their domain in the realm of incongruous things,
their dead petals folded over the edge, vaguely edifying:
as if our own skins could be laid out like washed clothes drying.

Licorne

1

Wild flowers stream upwards on the red ground
of her garden. Their stems are curved and slender
as the handles of umbrellas, drifting away, skybound.
I wish I knew their names and all their tender
ministrations, or could feel the delicate rain
they offer protection from. The lady's expression
is gently tolerant. The unicorn is there again.
She shows him the mirror with his reflection.
She tells him his horn is the emblem of singleness
in God and Christ. She tells him about the lion
that will devour him. He paws and scuffs her dress
entranced by its softness, its busy floral design.
He know he's in her realm. His body is as white
as hers is virginal. Her hand on his neck is light.

2

These are the feminine courtesies of tapestry.
This is the welcome she provides for him
within the sliding scale of her propriety
which is ethereal and fashionably slim.
You'd think it another romantic fantasy
of control but the strict language of love stuns
your senses. There is a rigour in the lazy
turn of her neck and in the floating patterns
of the flowers that is convincing. You know
the world is better like this, your heavy horn
more bearable, your body lighter, that you'll grow
more like the image that shows a smaller unicorn
beyond the glass, who has been smuggled through
to demonstrate that this, indeed, is you.

3

His unicorn ironies are useless in an enclosed
garden such as this. This is how things must be.
It is even flattering, the way he is posed,
a compliment to his supposed virility
which is flickering, fitful, dizzying, other, grand
as Beethoven with a fragile *es muss sein.*
So it must be. The touch of the lady's hand
is encouraging and there is something fine
about her breath. Her voice is musical:
a harp to his bagpipe bellow and squeak. He hears
it summon him by name. Irresistible.
He finds himself pricking up his ears.
He hears those airy cadenzas. She is chanting verses
from a book. He throws himself on her tender mercies.

4

Why should I, *he asks himself,* inhabit
a world of allegories? I was once a creature
as real as you, whose existence you'd do well to credit.
Like the weaver, I too was a child of nature
but imagination took me, made me elegant,
taught me the rules of courtly love. I could
unlearn them all and be as intelligent
as any other beast in the wild wood,
but even the language brims with courtesy,
its syntax runs through my entire being.
I am tamed, lady. It is our joint fantasy
that brings me to you under an all-seeing
weaver-god's protection, whose fine stitching
has made you grave and utterly bewitching.

5

The garden is mine. The flowers spiralling
upwards emanate from my desires. You are,
do not forget it, a guest to do my bidding.
Come here. Lie down. I see the frozen star
at the point of your horn. I will relieve you of it.
It's what you owe me. It is the tithe you pay
for being here. Do you imagine I profit
from your existence? I who, day after day,
must feed the garden with my energies?
You can make what you want of the wild wood
that you have ruined. And you can keep those elegies
which mean nothing to me or the neighbourhood.
It is, after all, your nature to deceive.
I'll let you know when it's time for you to leave.

Black Sea Sonnets

Palm

There is the sea, we say, as the wind
pushes if to and fro, and each time it lays
another open palm before us
it whisks it away. One day is like all days,
the same phrase sung by the same chorus.
In the distance the lights and cries
of a wedding, stray dogs in loose family groups.
It is as if the night were pinned
to the sky insecurely, not quite the right size.
And what might lie behind it? Brilliant loops
of naked stars cavorting and a moon full
of bad luck growing ever more silver. There
is something in the water beyond the pull
of tides, something released into the air.

Lake

And the little brown frogs plop into the lake
as if keeping time to footsteps. How still it is.
Acorns lie on the ground, the leaves are falling
so silently, so lightly. There is nothing to shake
the trees, only the nearby sea, the invisible cities
hidden under it, full of darkness and loss.
In the submarine city traffic is crawling
past paper-thin apartment blocks, across
wide boulevards, but here there is only the moment
before time begins. The water is smooth and tight
in the lake. The sea nearby is almost silent.
Water and water. And then the frog springs
and leaps with its tiny splash and time sings
for an instant as it might do this or any other night.

Speech

The noise of fear remains long after the cause;
becomes itself a cause, and habits die hard.
You hear it in the speeches, watch fraught slips
of paper circulate, or see a questioner pause
and remain silent. The Black Sea purses its lips
at the facing villas and draws us in to her
like a dull secret. Shall we walk in and stir
the waves a little? Pick a few cowries? Reward
ourselves for our exhaustion? Feed the dogs
that scamper about our feet? There are lists
to cover the darkest recesses of your heart
but the wind sweeps them away. What is it clogs
the arteries and blows the official files apart
reminding us the outside world exists?

Delta

Hour after hour, cruising through high reeds
in the Delta. Phalaropes, egrets, delicate
yellowish necks. Fishermen, cabins, then nothing.
More nothing. More reeds. The odd pocket
of humanity, then floating. Each channel breeds
an identical silence in regulation clothing.
Good to die here perhaps, or simply to dream
in the continuous sun that blisters our skin,
to move into an entropic state, to survive in
our own decay. Idyllic too: the stream
lapping at the boat with its tonnage of words,
the endless black coffee. We are part of the river,
drifting among spirits of pale waterbirds.
One should stay here, if possible, for ever.

Beach

Two figures on the beach in the dark.
A car cruises by. Two more figures approach.
Slurp, say the waves, licking at their feet.
Night shimmers and crackles with stars. Dogs bark
in the distance, sniffing the air with its sweet
tang of sufficiency. The moment is stable.
The sea frozen. Never again will it encroach
on the cities on its fringes. But underground
the faults widen and slide to a predictable
if imprecise rhythm, to a low rumbling sound
beneath the metro that precedes panic. One man
is making deals, another is counting names,
and the sea begins to move more subtly than
either can know, in tongues, with cold black flames.

Hospital

You press the button but the lift won't start
however you keep slamming at the door.
You must get out. The hospital needs treatment
more than its patients. There is a secret art
to finding the right staircase. Every floor
could be another. Your appointment
is with M.C. Escher, dying in a ward
suspended in a wing elsewhere. The lost
are fading into kindness or are restored
to a fading kind of health. We have crossed
some great divide into this. There is sea
in the walls, sea in the blood, in the head
of the man on the ventilator. The dead
sing down the lift shaft. The lift itself stands empty.

Sweet

There are places to get drunk in. The wedding night
at the hotel. The presidential villa with its terrace
overlooking the water. The bedroom with its freight
of sharp mosquitos. In the company of Cerberus,
the dog in the driveway, and his friends. We are alight
with dowsed bulbs and the television flickering
in the corner. It is inexpressibly sweet
all this, among the lost fireflies of a state
in its dotage or birth pangs, whichever it is,
waiting for hands or lips or languages to meet
in the lottery of improbabilities.
The sea is murmuring under its black wing.
The frogs by the lake hesitate, then fly
away, dropping like light rain from a clear sky.

Body

The spirit is compact with the body. This one
is seen by night, by a flickering television
that plays on the inside of the skull and in
the fingers, amplified through the heart.
A long way past twelve, new programmes begin
but none can keep spirit and body apart.
Pictures stutter, fizz into music, then slip
between the eyes. Voices, more voices. A curved
shadow turns to tears down a fingertip.
Regular news bulletins continue their well-preserved
list of disasters. The sea continues lapping
at the shore. Outside the window the dark
presses its face to the glass and starts tapping
out reminders, its eyes brilliant and stark.

Song

Inside every other is a you, and this you
is what I would sing, if I had a voice to sing it,
because the song would be poignant, pointed,
unmistakeable, rejoicing, eternal and blue,
the way a horn tails off into silence or an unlit
room. And I'd hear the Black Sea as it shunted
slowly to an fro, its joy made of desire,
of loss, and sheer astonishment. Perhaps
at its core, in its dying deep bed, it moans
and hums in a voice we can't hear, that laps
at the place where our hands were, where a silver wire
of foam creeps beneath the skin into the bones
and goes on living there, I don't know how,
but it's as if I heard that singing now.

The Matrix

*Also, in the ambience and the ethos of my birth and upbringing
there was an unconscious directing and moulding of my future life*
A Prevailing Wind: Memoirs of the Life of the Rev William Upchurch

Darling, out of what mould have we emerged
from our birth that we should speak as we do
in the moments we have? Can the story be true?
Has someone set us up? Could our paths have diverged
and gone separate ways once the course we have run
was determined? Is there a shape that is ours
and had to be once we had spent the first hours
in the cold matrix of the genes? What's done is done,
say the truisms, who rarely are wrong. Just yesterday
I was sitting with once-lovely Helen. I couldn't take
my eyes off the face in the skin and the trick
she must have mastered early of a delicate flick
of the eye that was for ever not sixty-five, and the grey
hair swinging across it as if she were half-awake,

like the unconscious directing perhaps of gravity
which was also directing the skin and the slow beat
of the heart in the fingers and the gradual loss of heat
in the flesh, with wonderful impassivity;
which is to say I wondered at it, as I do at my own
and at yours and the whole matrix thing, that scene
where Keanu Reeves floats in the air, guns blazing between
wide pillars and the brief moment of being is blown
open with special effects like a myth about winning
possession of space, time and death, and I trace
the path of the bullets in the air, seeking the holes
in our lives, in our curiously combined souls
which must somewhere have had a beginning
and come to this point in your hands and my eyes, in one space.

Cities

Good God, he says, looking at his watch.
Is that the time? The century ticks
inside their hearts. They feel the sun's light touch
on their foreheads. Raw vermilion bricks
blur and soften opposite. Now, where
were we? Was it this moment or the last
the sentence spoken was hung out to air?
And was it finished? A whole life flutters past
like a shadow, but do we know whose it is?

Everywhere broken voices, small talk of leaves
and flies. A piano treads and spins in
circles. He is stroking his unshaven chin.
She feels her back ache. Something deceives
the clock and expands in them like cities.

*

Sun in the city: high heat in the streets,
blinding exits from doorways, exhaust fumes
suddenly statuesque, walls in flat sheets
of uncanny thinness. The map assumes
an inward dimension, spreads into the lungs.
We eat the world and, over the years, become
like it, ascending the haunted concrete rungs
of ancient stairwells, passing our own children, dumb
on the landing in the shadows. In discreet squares,

on park benches, isolated moments
wait to be introduced to each other. They ache
for tenderness. And look, from under the pediments
we ourselves emerge, the pavements bake
in heat, and people are going about their affairs.

Three Separations

David and Ellen

Don't talk about it, do it, she said and turned
her face to the wall. David stared at the ceiling.
The space behind his eyes burned.

He was trying to locate an elusive natural feeling
somewhere in the halo of the lamp.
Her shoulder strap had slipped revealing

a patch of skin he wanted to touch with his damp
hot fingers. But the moment had passed. Hers, his,
both. They were stuck there in some kind of cramp.

Impossible to move without pain beyond the crisis,
impossible to imagine beyond it. As once before
a long time ago, in a shower of roses and lilies,

he had met her walking across a sunlit floor
having slept late. And it had been like rain,
or a gust of wind in a draught under the door

but brilliant and accompanied by pain.
Her body was still now, warm yet frozen.
It's what they'd woken to. How they'd remain.

Robert and Emily

When she reached for him under the covers
he seized her hand and squeezed it till it hurt.
It was a long time since they had become lovers

and now came the turning point, a plain curt
gesture. Enough was enough. No point now
in seductive candlelit evenings, pretending to flirt

in restaurants, no point in having a row
and breaking up in public, and no sense
in scoring points, in tears, not anyhow.

Something was leaking away in the tense
darkness. Robert and Emily. It was blood
of a sort, that deep pressing presence

they'd grown with and had long ago understood.
And so she turned away leaving a clear
space between them as, it now seemed, for good,

and in the darkness the faint noise of fear
began to buzz in their ears with a steep
tonal insistence as if their voices could appear

to haunt them just before they fell asleep.

Zoë and Neil

After the baby died it was as if her heart
had been drawn out on a string through her eyes,
and there was no more rest for them, together or apart.

Whose fault was it? Who should apologise
for the death of one so small? There was a lot
of it about, she read, enough death to surprise

the living. A baby would lie safe, you might think, in a cot
but the bad angel of breath may choose to spread
its suffocating wing over the very spot

the poor child occupies and so the child be dead.
So Zoë's thoughts turned round and round, until
her body rose and hovered and the wind took the head

through which that heart had leapt and made her ill.
The wind took her head, threw it in the air
and a man was there to catch it who was not Neil,

who could not be, as Neil saw to his despair.
They moved through the faint rooms they'd known
and eventually all the rooms were bare,

and Zoë flying ever further and Neil alone
while somewhere the enormous child rested
among others as enormous, once Zoë had flown

like a dirigible, light, and delicately breasted.

Shoulder

Goddess: her shoulder, her back, the round of her rump, I sing.
Though they sing themselves it is not in my language, this language,
But the language of life which is elsewhere, uninterpreted
And therefore incomprehensible and yet singing.

And though it is late, and once, whenever, it was younger,
Like you, Goddess, if you have any age, it is still the same
Shoulder and back and rump, which is hers and the language's
And wholly impersonal, the idea of a back and a shoulder,

And how I shudder to touch it, the shudder of pleasure
And affection, the shudder of itself, which, like a word,
Vibrates in its space, like her breath, which is lovely
And personal, in this room with its clock, with its word.

What is love, Goddess? You whom I address with humble
Generic precision, are you capable of answering
In the language of life? Am I capable of writing
Or thinking or feeling the space of the word?

It is Saturday, Tuesday, Friday, the weather goes on,
I can hear people speaking. There are bombs and bullets,
The usual business of war, which is rarely interrupted.
It is Wednesday and Thursday and Monday.

In a Sunday of the mind our bodies roll closer
And each part feels like a morning, an afternoon, an evening.
I want to sing the body on terrible Sunday,
On disastrous Monday and Tuesday, the days of my life.

Retro-futuristic

It is cruel to feel the climax of depression on approaching
your own land, and to see it as a grim retro-futuristic mirage.
ANTONIA APOSTOLOVA

Everywhere in the city, gangs of labourers
are digging up brown fields where banks and shops
once stood in a lost quarter of mirages
full of phantom metro stations, bus stops,
news-stands and fast-food outlets. Great white
concrete towers shimmer and vanish at once
in constantly flashing beams of sunlight.
A neon sign hangs in a cloud. Empty carriages
on the railway bridge are almost transparent
as they speed past, still accelerating
into the outskirts through inner-city slums
where invisible workers gather, patiently waiting.

It is cruel to feel the depression rising, and harder still
to maintain belief in what's gone and never was,
a notional history of the soul, like some urban infill
between a more concrete emptiness one daren't
demolish for fear of losing everything.
It is cruel to wake without visible neighbours
in disappearing apartments to the faint buzz
of houseflies feeding on mountains of damp stinking
refuse. How can one live here? How to define
a space among illusions? An aeroplane curves
between buildings. The calendar says 1989.
There is nowhere to go except the future,

or down to the cinema where they are playing
Blade Runner again. There is Harrison Ford
hanging on for dear life while Rutger Hauer
turns to stone. There is something dismaying
about the scenario, like listening to a cracked record.
And then the beautiful white dove of the soul
rises into perpetual rain above the tower
with its half-recognised high-tech furniture.
The buildings throng with stucco cherubim.
It is Sofia, Tirana, Bucharest, New York. The rain
washes away the rubbish. There is a tight scroll
of froth in the street. Certainly it is grim.

Climate

The sky is broken. There is the usual scud
of dense cloud: showers, lightning, a shower
and then the cycle begins again. Each hour
is a new foray into a thin skim of mud
beside the river. Ducks huddle under leaves
then waddle out into brief sunshine. Nowhere
will you find any fixed point that might bear
your weight or even your spirits. Nothing receives
the imprint of your shoe. It is England of course,
not one of the dependable climates. Things fly
in muscular gusts: flags, bunting, news-sheets.
It is as if there were some irresistible force
blowing us over into a strange new century
that billows beyond us, between our thin heart-beats.

Decades

First Decade: To be Recited at Times of Trouble

The best lack all conviction while
   The worst have gone the extra mile,
   And must, therefore, arrive there first
   Where worst is best and best is worst.

Justice lays a clutch of eggs
   Out of which climb
   Creatures with a thousand legs
   Given the time.

Chickens roasting on their spits
   Are genuinely thrilled to bits.
   It's good to hear the customer speak
   So warmly of their curve of beak.

Revenge is a dish best eaten cold.
   You sit so long at the table waiting to be served,
   But someone eventually brings you
   The meal you have deserved.

You could fuel an airforce with that hatred.
   Watch how a single aircraft taxis
   Across a crooked runway
   On its mischievous axis.

Open the box and out fly all the names
   Of despair loudly caterwauling,
   Immediately to engage in their favourite games
   Of hyperbole and name-calling.

Pity wears too many faces. She complains
   Of exhaustion and fever,
   It seems her destiny is to suffer shooting pains
   Every morning, forever.

Genocide
     Has no funny side,
     Nor can survival
     Brook a rival.

The peculiar carpentry of the coffin
     Constructed by a gun
     Ensures that it falls apart the moment it's laid in the ground,
     And yet fits everyone.

When God at first made man
     Having a glass of blessings standing by
     It seemed a good idea and, after all,
     It does behove a deity to try.

Second Decade: The People of the Book

The People of the Book
    React with bookish fury,
    Adding another chapter to
    The troubled tale of Jewry.

It doesn't take much,
    It never takes more
    Than a delicate touch
    And some blood on the floor.

It's not a matter
    Of life or death,
    The old man assures us
    With his last breath.

They were too meek.
    They were compliant.
    Says the Holocaust Dwarf
    To his grandson, the Giant.

Between Chagall and Chaim Soutine
    There's room left for debate:
    And on such grounds of argument
    We may well found a state.

In creating a state as a refuge
    They might have foreseen
    That they'd carry with them the dust
    Of the places they'd been.

Once the displaced had settled down
    And their pulses had stopped racing
    They spread their belongings out on the lawn
    And set about others' displacing.

When God is under the weather
    He looks upon his chosen,
    Shrugs with disgust and leaves them
    In the desert, frozen.

Under the magnifying glass
Toothpicks become stakes,
And people in their hundreds die
Because a man's tooth aches.

Life is nasty, brutish and short
So what harm in making it shorter?
All it takes is a bit of paste
Or the distant sound of a mortar.

Third Decade: On Trespasses

When they scored they bent
    And kissed the eighteen-yard-line
    As if the pitch were sacred
    And scoring a sign.

Mahmoud, Jamal and Hicham,
    The girls arrive and press
    Your lips; sleek Ruth, bright Hannah
    and Judith in her Sabbath dress.

Europa has a party and invites
    All ranks of city-dwellers
    Into her penthouse bedrooms
    And filthy cellars.

There is a long music
    That moves in a slow stream
    Within our blood. To wake from it
    Is like breaking a dream.

God does not forget,
    So how can you ask of a man
    To repeat the same mistake
    Time and again?

We do not inhabit land,
    Land inhabits us:
    On that point our scribes
    Are quite unanimous.

Great leaders with beautiful manners
    Have mastered the trick
    Of command. Speaking softly is hopeless
    Without a very big stick.

They hurt our pride and broke
    The neck of our god under their yoke.
    Into the void his head falls
    For ever, and his voice calls.

Believe unto death! they cry
    As they strap on the belt
    Of death. Believe! they cry
    As their bones melt.

The defeated have ceased to exist.
    One cannot stop existing.
    Once the living have been killed
    The dead can start enlisting.

Fourth Decade: Editorials

The wind blew hard. There was
    The usual rain of blood.
    The *Apocalyptic Herald* landed
    On the mat with a dull thud.

Major world figures made speeches,
    The press bit its nails,
    As the flawed engine of Good Will
    Ran off the rails.

World is stranger and suddener
    Than leader writers think.
    You can't tie it down in its trolley
    With a dose of printer's ink.

One after another they frowned
    And spoke as if their hearts
    Were laden down by what they had
    To say in their various parts.

Something corrosive was eating away
    At the fabric of the tongue.
    The breath froze in the mouth of the word.
    Alarm bells rung.

So much righteousness
    Concentrated on a page:
    One item tagged onto another,
    Rage on rage.

There are things that happen,
    And there is the news,
    A whole electric industry
    On a single fuse.

Listen to the incidental music
    Of what happens as it dies
    In the ear, and beyond it the sound
    Of faint, barely audible cries.

The camera's brief intimacies.
>One glass eye must serve all those
>Who crowd in to touch death
>At the point the lids close.

Death's production values
>Are low-tech and demeaning.
>You need to frame things properly
>To give them meaning.

Fifth Decade: The Palace of Art

In a classical porch two angels
    Are steadily beating their God.
    You must train your deities properly.
    No point sparing the rod.

St Veronica lends her hankie
    To the fallen. Next day
    she opens it up: Oh my god!
    I have taken his face away.

A wheel on a pole. A raven.
    The crowd has formed a ring.
    In the centre: death.
    And still they keep coming.

Always this bare hillside and the crowd
    huddling and thinking aloud,
    thoughts that collect in the valley beneath
    with folded spectacles, shoes, gold teeth.

It is awfully black down there,
    And their limbs are terribly bent:
    How lifelike the darkness is
    We seemed to be doomed to invent.

Hell is muscular and crowded
    Like a gym where the demons work out
    Their frustrations on apparatus
    Unhindered by rust or by doubt.

God slides down the chute of his robe:
    His body seems almost to float.
    The late romantic chorus of love
    Belts on in full throat.

We watch the universe collapsing
    About the victim's head.
    The living are turned away from us.
    Not so the dead.

Soldiers asleep, he stands
    Stiff backed: his eyes burn.
    Resurrection begins.
    Now it is our turn.

You put your fingers in the wound
    Gingerly, since you doubt.
    The problem is not so much poking it in
    As getting the damn thing out.

Three Poems for Sebastião Salgado

Preface to an Exhibition

How beautiful suffering is, and how sad:
As the waste flies the wind catches.
The wasted drift among dispatches,
Above the debris, the dirt and the spent matches,
Well-lit but ill-clad.

How beautiful suffering is, and how wild
When the dead scream as loud as the dying
And the cracked glass of the terrifying
Intruder shows the dead child flying
Past the living child.

How statuesque the lost are, how well defined
Each graceful gesture of grief,
Each moment as perfect and brief
As the burning curl of a napalmed leaf
Or a motion of the mind.

The pity, the beauty, the horror and the calm,
The flight of birds in a swirl of smoke,
The deafening noise, the brilliant stroke,
The click of a button like a tender joke
With its offer of balm.

How beautiful suffering is and how soon:
The sense of home as a distant speck,
And mud and night and an endless trek,
The beauty of the rifle's slender neck
In the light of the moon.

How beautiful suffering is as a theme
Where the eye shuts like a shutter
On blood in a gutter
Or moves like a knife through melted butter
Or the dark through a dream.

How beautiful suffering is, and how numb,
Where the moving are stilled
Where no one is killed
And the sound is your breathing forever distilled
And the loud are the dumb.

The wicked boy by the pylons

I am the wicked boy, I walk by pylons, my scowl
Is a terminus, my eyes are beyond you,
I am Rimbaud and the dead, and the black faced owl
In the ruined shed, I am the whoo

In your *who is it*, I am lost for ever in sand,
In the industrial wasteland of the desert, grey
As the sky, as this, my very own wicked hand.
Will you take it and dance with me today

In the sand by the pylons where the shadows cross?
Will your smile heal me and swallow me whole?
Will your pity negate my eyes with its pathos?
Will you erase entirely my wholly wicked soul?

I am the lost boy, the sick boy, the deaf dumb
Malevolence I once met in the street
And became. Let me teach you therefore. Come
With me. Feel my hot head, feel my body heat.

Water

The hard beautiful rules of water are these:
That it shall rise with displacement as a man
does not, nor his family. That it shall have no plan
or subterfuge. That in the cold, it shall freeze;
in the heat, turn to steam. That it shall carry disease
and bright brilliant fish in river and ocean.
That it shall roar or meander through metropolitan
districts whilst reflecting skies, buildings and trees.

And it shall clean and refresh us even as we slave
over stone tubs or cower in a shelter or run
into the arms of a loved one in some desperate quarter
where the rats too are running. That it shall have
dominion. That it shall arch its back in the sun
only according to the hard rules of water.

Account

When the sacred being had said what he had to say
They set off as ordered into the autumn sunlight.
It was neutrally brilliant, a perfectly calm day
And business was brisk at the appointed site.
The mind struggled, as it usually did, to write
Letters of dismissal, memos of loss or delay,
When all it wanted to note was how it was all right
With the account healthy and time enough to pay.

But it wasn't and wouldn't be when phones were ringing
With all the lost messages, most of them much too brief,
Full of exploded phrases and broken sentences.
But the sacred being had written off their absences.
His accounts were already balanced out with grief
And he bade the heavenly choir continue singing.

Arrival

Finally we arrived at the city of silence,
enormous, high-walled, its furious traffic lights
signalling in panic. The streets were covered over
in thick rugs. It was a place without doors, a series
of moving mouths.
                    Their eyes, of course, spoke volumes,
vast encyclopaedias. There was little light reading.
Their white gloves fluttered before them
with grotesquely dancing fingers.

It was written that all this should be as it was.
Their thought-crimes, hand-crimes, and heart-crimes
were listed in long numbered chapters.
Policemen pulled faces or pointed at notices.
The civic authorities were sleeping in the park.
DO NOT DISTURB, said the signs.
ASK NO AWKWARD QUESTIONS.

The rest went on feeding and breeding.
They were planting tongues in the cemetery,
thick flowering shrubs of silence.

Tent

The cool blue tent is a jag on the red sand
among nineteen types of palm
in an early phase of night.
The tick of insects at the palm tree's root
is the sole music: a beetle glooms through the leaves.
You wave away a fly in the iron dark of the tent.

Tent is a beacon, tent is a harbinger.
It peaks on the ribbed sand like a sign.
It is your clown's hat, your little scoop of night.
Beyond the trees the skyscrapers huddle,
their lifts tingling with muzak
as they zip up the sides of the buildings
and seal them off from moon and stars.

Where is she, your love? It is lonely on the planet,
though the tent is cool and blue and means you well.

The Morpheus Annotations

(for Katharina Hacker)

Morpheus

The calls of Morpheus, once irregular, grow
still more irregular. You sense him leaving
by the window or the door and follow
his mocassins into the hall, sieving
light from dark, no longer quite believing
in his efficient ministrations in the hollow
parts of night, but he is gone, beyond retrieving,
with his moth-wing lashes. Then you too go,

into the kitchen or lie on the settee to watch
the dying loose flickers of the television,
its alien arctic ice-fields, its comforts such
as they are, lulling you with faint derision,
while Morpheus sweeps up the black snow of sleep
which once was lent to you, but not to keep.

*

The whole universe is packed with sleep so tight
you can hardly move an atom through its bulk.
For each short day, there are great fields of night
where a god might take offence, creep off and sulk
or bury his head in acres of black silk
to be consoled by the indeterminate flight
of his own dreams, his blood as thick as milk,
his veins heavy, his heart an ammonite.

Morpheus taps his fingers on the sill
outside the window. The all-night news is lawn
beneath his feet. Dewdrops are beginning to spill
into his eyes. He goes for a piss at dawn
in the bathroom of his consciousness
then, hearing birds sing, slowly begins to dress.

Mnemon

He'd forget his head if it wasn't screwed on. Awake
at last he checks the list by the bed that had kept him awake
for hours last night. This morning a customer calls
with a problem and he spends the day dealing with phone calls.
Remember, they tell him, remember the chair she sat in,
something burned on the water, something in satin,
or samite, or something. He dips the hazel wand of his dreamy side
into that unknown something. There are boxes inside
boxes down there and, dreaming them, they come up
drenched and clear. At night he writes it all up
in a ledger, makes lists for the morning. There is something
missing each time. It's his head or something,
it seems to have come unscrewed. Now, where did he leave
the screwdriver? He asks his wife. She tells him: leave
me alone or I'll call the police. I know you, he protests,
we were sharing a bed just now... His protests
fall on deaf ears. She disappears into a barge
on a something river. Into something very like a barge.

Sisyphus

When Sisyphus enters the hotel
he drops his bags. He rings the bell.
This is, he checks, Pensione Hell?

Charon emerges through a door.
It is all that and something more,
What can we do for the signor?

Sisyphus glances at the stairs.
You could relieve me of my cares
by taking my baggage. *Your affairs*

are strictly your own. I assume
you'll want the very topmost room.
Here are the keys. It's like a tomb

up there and Sisyphus sleeps alone,
or would if he could. He's stretched out prone
and wide awake. He hears the stone

muttering in its metal box
sealed in the biggest case. He blocks
his ears. The bed he lies on gently rocks.

Hotel life. Baggage. Minibar.
TV. Remote control. They are
migrating souls who've travelled far

to get to places such as these
as if they cured some vague disease
but were themselves diseased. The keys

are weighing down his pockets. Night
comes on suddenly like a flashlight
or mysterious loss of appetite.

The bedside phone. The trouser press
in the cupboard. Emptiness
in drawers and bins. Last known address.

The stone rolls out along the bed
and comes to rest beside his head.
He thinks, therefore he must be, dead.

The bill arrives some six months later.
The room yawns open as a crater.
The stone comes down the elevator.

Elpenor

Elpenor? We were fond of Elpenor.
Generous, kind, intelligent and brave
    Elpenor, in company, at dinner,
In the bar. There were days he didn't shave,
    When his embrace was abrasive yet gentle,
When he looked at us from beyond the grave
    In a reassuring, faintly parental
Fashion, as if to say, this too is all right,
    As if death itself were somehow sentimental
And lost; when he stumbled through streets at night,
    A familiar arm round a friend's shoulder, blinking
At the world before him under a dull streetlight
    Recalling aloud other nights of such drinking
As is the way with drinkers, and his eyes
    Swam off into themselves, his clothes stinking
Of spilled wine, his hands touching the unzipped flies
    Of his pants, and there would be a marvellous
Story he could tell coherently enough to surprise
    His companions, whose love of him was jealous
And literally supportive, for he too bore
    Them gladly, an inspissated Daedalus
Of rhetorical devices. Ah, Elpenor,
    They sighed, he was human but could speak
Like an angel, in exemplary manner,
    And they remembered his love of Greek,
His vulnerable mouth, his once-slender
    Body, his moustache (long gone) and his sleek
Aesthetic gait, and felt unutterably tender.
    Nightly he would sup at Circe's in Soho,
Or the Colony Room then go on a bender
    At all the little pubs, and everyone would know
Elpenor and greet him and help him along,
    And women kissed him full-heartedly as though
They recognised their loss in his, their wrong
    In his helplessness, knowing him once adept
At all they loved, at playfulness and song,
    And watched him, heart-in-mouth, as he leapt
Blindly into the underworld, his old body crumpled,
    Their voices soft as he breathed out and slept.

Minotaur in the Metro

I have seen them myself, heard the sound of their hooves
moving down the platform like cattle, driven
down tunnels, weeping, snuffling, bellowing,
their hairy wrists awkwardly stuffed into sleeves,
their lost eyes tiny and furious, rimmed with fur,
framed by spectacles. They clutch briefcases
tightly to their chests, as if they were children
hugging some battered toy for security
and are swept by harsh winds down corridors.
Slim women in pale dresses, faintly Chekhovian
introspective types, demand their attention.
They take a hairy book from the depths
of their cases and cover themselves for fear
their expressions might betray them. The whole train
is thick with the smell of them, the sound of their breathing.

Sometimes I hear their otherness breathing
gently down my windpipe, travelling on the ghost train
of whatever passes through the blood like a fear
without an object, seeking the unknown depths
of itself, and then my body is all attention,
a terrible bull in an orderly Chekhovian
orchard, watching for movement in the corridors
of the house at the end of the garden, wired for security,
with its freight of grown-up familiar children.
I personally have owned and known briefcases
that demanded obedience, have felt the lice on my fur
gather and revolt, have carefully studied my sleeves
with their attached appendages, heard myself bellowing
silently in fields only dreamt of, where cattle are driven
to slaughter in underground mazes on delicate hooves.

Ariadne observed by the Eumenides

A

Whose heart would not be moved by the plight of this woman,
Cheated and abandoned on Naxos, poor soul, having given
Her heart like the others before her, whole femme-loads deserted.
Who'd not be driven to fury by evil- or faint-hearted
Wooers and louses? Who after all are the masters?
The sailors? Bull-slayers? I tell you: all men are bastards.

B

One winter night by the bus stop I saw a girl crying,
Her make-up quite smudged with her tears. I was dying
To seek out the arsehole and hex him. Her heart was a broken
Axle, her chassis was holed, there was about her a terrible shaking.
She hovered before me like a wisp of fog in the fury
Of the downpour and how I longed to do him an injury.

A

I saw her too. I could look clean through her trembling body,
Cities were alight there, her organs were screaming. Had he
Appeared that moment, I would have torn him asunder.
Can anyone explain why men are happy to slander
The tenderest feelings and leave behind them such agony?
Let's fuck him up now and haunt him to buggery.

B

Disaster will come to him too in due season,
Any day now, on that hardly distant horizon.
Let him arrive there. Let her mourning be beautiful.
I hear drums and leopards. Some gods at least can be useful.
Bacchus will look after her, from now on, for ever.
The rat's almost home. I can just see the face of his father.

Charon

Dans le vieux parc, solitaire et glacé
I saw a couple pass and move away.

There was the pond, the little boats were moored
Along the edge, bobbing and faintly bored.

The boatman sat by his hut, reading a fat
Slab of a book with an embossed title. That

Was all. The couple were lost to view. The moon
Silvered and sharpened as if all misfortune

Were concentrated in it, somewhere over
And above the hut. The book with its cover

Closed. Charon got up. My love stood out clear
On the far side, calling but I couldn't hear

Her. The trees too closed. The water grew
Rapidly colder, the sky a deeper blue.

Three Pieces for Puppetry

1 *The Garden of Earthly Delights*

In the garden of earthly delights a maid sings
in the moonlight and hands escape from their
supporting roles
to act out erotic fantasies as lovers or wings,
or fish in sensually drifting shoals
of light and coloured air.

A frogman appears in the deep like a drowned
monster pulling faces through his goggles.
A plump red heart
floats above a manequin to the sound
of drums. Two old grotesques start
a fight. One struggles

with the other, they knock their heads together,
rolling over and over. It's all about money
and lust – what else is there?
Scraps of cloth, bits of old shoe leather,
stuff from the junkshop, all things spare
and cheap and funny.

All this in a tiny theatre the size of a man's head,
a man with a big head, a completely outrageous
capacious and outsize
head who is telling a story composed of fraying thread
held together by conventions, tricks and lies,
the discarded pages

of ancient directories to the business of living.
The grown ups are being graceful to amuse
their notional child.
They are trying to impose order on the unforgiving
minute. Like poetry, it is the formal dance of the wild,
news which stays news.

Fancy having a hand up your backside
all your life! To be so filled with Hand
that hand is all in all.
This is a religious proposition. You're tied
by the puppeteer's laws. By them you stand
or (more probably) fall.

It may be only convention but I'm filled
with hand as with holy spirit, am wholly possessed
by another's will.
Perhaps I am merely a helpless child
born without legs, helplesly overdressed
and terminally ill.

The hand that rocks the cradle rocks me
to kingdom come. Do I have an identity
I may call mine?
Is there a centre? My author shocks me
with his terrible lack of pity.
Is it by design

or by some Darwinian joke I have survived
so far? Do I believe in that moody
God with cold stumpy digits?
What makes me cruel? What makes me hide
within myself and beat poor Judy?
Why do I get the fidgets

and make ridiculous noises some mistake
for wit? Is the world like me? Excuse
the rhetoric – I know
we are different but which is real, which is fake?
The world or my self? If it's me, then whose
words are these? whose thoughts flow

through my papier-mâché head? whose lust
blows me out, expands me inch by inch?
What is it to play glove
to a God whose own essence is dust?
Does God at all care for Mister Punch?
Could this be love?

It is an ordinary dream and a mundane urge
the dream contains. It is romance
in the pleasure dome,
a sense of falling off the undefined verge
of the world, or taking part in a dance
in an aerodrome

while bombers approach down the runway
droning and darkening the sky.
It is the ridiculous
limb movements, the twitches, the mad gay
leaps in the air, the lips going dry,
the painful rictus

in mid-scream, the unsayable words
that are left behind after the flight
has landed or
is taking off in a shower of birds
when the sky goes black as night
or a closed door.

It is the terrible hunger unsatisfied
by the nature goddess, the weird
acrobatic judder
in the spine, it is the voiceless bride
in the cathedral waiting for Bluebeard,
the mad cow's udder.

It's the magic of moonlight and rain
and the weightless heart bursting
in the wooden breast.
It is the moth's wings beating in vain
at the window, the desire, the thirsting
and flying. And all the rest.

Elephant

Imagine this: somewhere, in a far-off land,
you are reincarnated in the form of an elephant,
ponderous, grey, inscrutable, all your old silkiness
hosed off you abruptly. Now you aspire
to wisdom and gravity: frivolity you abhor,
all social graces you dismiss as farce.

It is as if you were watching an old Whitehall Farce
with Brian Rix blundering about in an England
of seaside postcards. The things you used to abhor
as vulgarity, though beneath your dignity as an elephant
seem oddly apt now. The little men who aspire
to vast women in one-piece stripy swimsuits are lost in the silkiness

of the sea where other leviathans sport. It is the only silkiness
allowed you. That and soft rain. Meanwhile the farce
you're engaged in lumbers on. The little men aspire:
the fat ladies in spotty knickers conspire and billow. The land
is all ruts and scrub, which is small beer to an elephant
but not likeable either. And there are creatures to abhor:

scrofulous monkeys, bloated crocodiles, foul-breathed bears. To abhor
is to avoid, to laugh is to snort, to loathe is to sneer. O silkiness!
O crêpe-de-chine! Sweet flim-flam! O delicate elephant
of the imagination! Dream on, big boy. Consider the farce
of the universe with its bumbling planets. See meteors land
with an almight cosmic thump. What is it to aspire

to sky-dust, moonshine, deodorant, hairspray? Aspire
to be an atom drifting in desolate glory. Do not abhor
a vacuum. Be not like nature. Be spirit not body, air not land.
Inhabit a galaxy of conceptual silkiness
where Venus is disembodied desire, where farce
turns to wit or light irony, as befits an elephant

with memories of lightness. For what is an elephant
but condensation of cloud? Is it not made to aspire
to lightning and cloudburst somewhere beyond the farce
of sheer tonnage? What is there, after all, to abhor?
Is the elephant's hide not a hornier silkiness?
Is his bulk not a balloon lilting above the land

like a brilliant thought to whose silkiness anyone might aspire?
Don't we love and abhor death? Is not the elephant
the image of corporeality in a land of fury and farce?

Wasp

Their truly horrible softness seems not to bother them,
nor their lack of mobility. They really are very slow
and fearful of perfectly ordinary things such as me.
What harm do I do them as I blow
on a whim through the window, lighter than a bee
or mayfly with my superior aerodynamic system?

My small sharp voice is as nothing to theirs,
their slow, billowing, mountaineous exhalations,
their spitting, the low dull explosions of their lips.
They are insensible to my more eloquent orations.
I slip between them like a speedboat among ships,
my tiny motor whirring with fine expensive hairs.

And think of the food they put down! Fair enough,
they are large, their requirements such as they are,
but the copiousness of their appetite would appal
the most generous of gods with a taste for the bizarre.
It is, I can tell you, illuminating to crawl
across their tables at mealtimes and gawp at the stuff.

Conspicuous consumption? Whoever invented
the phrase deserves a medal. Spot on, I'd say.
I like to get them ruffled, to raise their hackles
and send the slimebags on their graceless way
with a flea (or wasp) in the ear. Of all God's miracles
they are possibly the least. Their heavily scented

carcasses are an offence to the senses. Were I lord
of the universe I'd boil them down for glue,
use them for something or stop their mouths with wax.
The beautiful would inherit the earth along with the true
and our lot would be kicking their heels down the barracks
with a couple of them to amuse us, should we get bored.

Endragoblins

(for Olivia Cole)

You little green friend, read my father
from Dan Dare. No, *fiend*, I told him
The endragoblins were at it again,
monkeying with the language.
The Mekon sat in his saucer,
his green eyes bulging with venom.
The Eagle had landed. My father
was busy with the endragoblins
who populated every available nook of the universe,
calling to my father on his dying planet.

Winter Wings

(Wymondham Abbey)

How brilliantly the sun
for a moment strides
through the glass
then hides
in deep
recesses
in the very aisles
it so briefly caresses,

so the heart stops and restarts
without noticing
it has stopped:
a swing
lurching,
an eye lost
in mid-blink, dark birds
in full-flight, swimming through dust.